Nonprofit Law

A Practical Guide to Legal Issues for Nonprofit Organizations

Willard L. Boyd III, Editor

Nonprofit Organizations Committee

AMERICAN BAR ASSOCIATION
Business Law Section

Cover design by Cathy Zaccarine/ABA Design

Printed in the United States of America.

21 20 19 18 5 4 3 2

ISBN: 978-1-63425-949-1

Contents

Preface

We in the United States are fortunate to have many nonprofits providing valuable services in their communities. Given the limited resources of many charitable nonprofits, attorneys who serve on boards of nonprofits or are contacted by someone affiliated with a nonprofit often are asked to provide advice with regard to a nonprofit legal issue. For many of these attorneys, this may be the first time they have considered such an issue in the nonprofit context.

This book was developed from a series of webinars sponsored by the Nonprofit Organizations Committee of the ABA Business Law Section called "Nonprofit Law for the 'Non' Nonprofit Attorney." The webinar series is intended to provide some basic information and guidance on legal topics that commonly arise for nonprofits.

The webinar series has alternated each year as a three-part series, which focuses on the areas of nonprofit formation, tax exemption, and governance, and a two-part series, which focuses on issues relating to formation documents, governance policies, and applications for tax-exempt status and Form 990 information filings.

This book covers the formation, tax, governance, and documentation issues covered in the webinar series and addresses some other areas, including mergers and sale of assets of nonprofits as well as dissolution of nonprofits. Like the webinar series, this book is not intended to be a source of specific legal advice or of solutions to specific legal issues, but instead to provide basic information and guidance that may be helpful in becoming conversant on a matter when issues arise.

The following individuals have been presenters for the Nonprofit Law for the "Non" Nonprofit Attorney webinar series and prepared the presentations upon which part of this book is based: Lisa A. Runquist, Michael

E. Malamut, Jeannie C. Frey, Cynthia M. Rowland, Stephen M. Clarke, Ingrid Mittermaier, Rosemary E. Fei, Eric K. Gorovitz, Henry Lesser, and Willard L. Boyd III.

Special thanks and appreciation are owed to the following individuals who assisted with the editing of this book: Lisa A. Runquist, Northridge, CA, Michael E. Malamut, Boston, MA, Jeannie C. Frey, Chicago, IL, Cynthia M. Rowland, San Francisco, CA, Stephen M. Clarke, Washington, D.C., and Ingrid Mittermaier, San Francisco, CA.

Willard L. Boyd III
Des Moines, Iowa

Introduction

This book was prepared to assist attorneys who represent nonprofit organizations. This book is not intended to provide an extensive review or analysis of nonprofit issues, but is instead for the attorney who does not regularly practice in the area of nonprofit law and seeks a general understanding of issues common to nonprofits. Because this book is intended to provide an overview of the law with regard to particular issues, it provides limited statutory and regulatory citations. The reference materials listed in Appendix C provide more detailed analysis and citations.

As discussed throughout this book, many of the legal requirements imposed on nonprofits are based on state nonprofit corporation law. Each state's nonprofit corporation act is unique, so it is important that the attorney become familiar with the attorney's state nonprofit corporation act. The Nonprofit Organizations Committee of the ABA Business Law Section has developed model nonprofit corporation acts over the years that have been the basis for many state nonprofit corporation acts. The Revised Model Nonprofit Corporation Act of 1988, which was adopted by many states, was replaced by the Model Nonprofit Corporation Act, Third Edition, in 2008 (MNCA). The MNCA reflects the latest trends in nonprofit corporation laws and is therefore referenced throughout this book.

This book is organized in a manner similar to the webinar series upon which it is based.

Chapter 1 reviews some basic questions an attorney should ask a client when advising on nonprofit issues, whether the attorney is asked to help form a new nonprofit corporation or advise on some other nonprofit matter.

Chapter 2 addresses issues relating to formation and describes important documents that are part of the formation process, including articles of incorporation and bylaws.

Chapter 3 focuses on taxation issues with a focus on the types of federal tax exemptions that are available under the Internal Revenue Code, the classifications of nonprofits with tax-exempt status under section 501(c)(3), and the application process for federal tax-exempt status. Chapter 3 also summarizes the requirements associated with the information reporting filings (Form 990) required of tax-exempt entities. Finally, the chapter provides a summary overview of some other tax issues that can arise for tax-exempt entities including private inurement and benefit, unrelated business income tax, the prohibition on nonprofits with tax-exempt status under section 501(c)(3) with regard to political campaigns and limits imposed on these types of entities with regard to legislative lobbying.

Chapter 4 addresses governance matters and describes the individuals involved in the governance of a nonprofit corporation as well as the fiduciary duties imposed on the board of directors. This chapter summarizes some of the protections available to directors in the form of state and federal liability shields, indemnification, and directors and officers' liability coverage. Chapter 4 also reviews the impact of the Form 990 on governance as well describes board policies that help an organization ensure good governance. The chapter addresses the issues that arise when an attorney for the nonprofit also serves as a member of the board of directors of the nonprofit. Finally, Chapter 4 discusses keys to effective board service as well as describes steps to be taken for corporate housekeeping.

Chapter 5 focuses on other matters that often arise in representation of a nonprofit and includes discussion on subsidiaries of nonprofits, the merger, sale of assets and other entity combinations involving nonprofits, and dissolution of nonprofits.

The appendices include a checklist for articles of incorporation and bylaws, a list of tax exemptions under the Internal Revenue Code, as well as resource materials that can provide more detailed information on the subject matter provided in this book.

Introduction: Some Basic Questions

1

There are some basic questions that must be considered when advising a client on nonprofit issues. A nonprofit corporation generally is, in many respects, similar to a for-profit corporation, but there are important differences between the two types of entities. In addition, the concept of a nonprofit organization covers a wide variety of organizations that have significant differences among them. The financial viability of a nonprofit is also an important consideration. As a result, when a client requests that the attorney form a new nonprofit or advise on some other nonprofit legal matter, there are several important questions to consider.

WHAT KIND OF "NONPROFIT"?

The most common form of nonprofit organization—and the type that is the main focus of this book—is the nonprofit corporation, which typically is created pursuant to a state nonprofit corporation act. Other forms of nonprofit organizations include limited liability companies, unincorporated nonprofit associations, and charitable trusts, which are briefly addressed in this book.

A nonprofit corporation has many characteristics that are similar to a for-profit corporation. Like a for-profit corporation, a nonprofit corporation first comes into existence when the articles of incorporation are filed with the appropriate secretary of state's office and has similar entity attributes, including perpetual duration, the power to sue or be sued, and the power to hold and transfer property in the corporate name. Also like a for-profit corporation, a nonprofit corporation provides certain protections for its members, directors, officers, and volunteers from the debts and liabilities of the corporation.

Although a nonprofit corporation can look quite similar to a for-profit corporation, there are significant differences. Most importantly, unlike a for-profit corporation, there is no equity ownership in a majority of nonprofit corporations, and no profits are to be distributed. If there are any earnings, they generally are retained or used by the entity for its nonprofit purposes.

The fact that an organization is a nonprofit does not mean it is charitable. Most nonprofits are charitable, but many other nonprofits are organized for noncharitable purposes, such as professional associations and affinity groups. The key is that no profits are distributed to the members or managers of the organization.

IS THE NONPROFIT TAX-EXEMPT?

People often think nonprofits are always exempt from federal income tax, state income tax, sales tax, and property tax. This is not the case. It is important to recognize that the terms "nonprofit" and "tax-exempt" are not synonymous. The mere fact a nonprofit corporation exists under a state nonprofit corporation act does not mean the entity has federal income tax-exempt status or that it is exempt from state income taxes, sales taxes, or property taxes. Instead, an important "second" step that must be taken as part of the formation process—after incorporating and completing other organizational activities—is to obtain tax-exempt status in accordance with applicable requirements under the Internal Revenue Code, which may include the filing of a tax exemption application with the Internal Revenue Service (IRS) as well as to take other steps at the state and/or county levels to obtain tax-exempt status at those levels.

Without obtaining tax-exempt status, a nonprofit corporation is "taxable" and subject to the regular corporate income tax rates.

WHAT IS MEANT BY TAX-EXEMPT STATUS?

There are different types of tax exemptions. The main type relates to the organization obtaining exemption from federal income tax, which, as noted above, may require an application to the IRS. Depending on the state of incorporation, there may be exemption application processes that must be followed in order for the organization's income to be exempt under state law. For example, there is a process that must be followed in California in order to be exempt from that state's franchise income tax.

In addition, it is possible a nonprofit corporation may be exempt from other taxes, such as sales tax and property taxes. These types of exemptions are not always available, and even if available, are typically not automatic, vary from state to state, and may require application to the applicable governing authority.

WHAT IS THE FEDERAL AND STATE OVERSIGHT FOR THE NONPROFIT?

A nonprofit corporation typically is subject to regulatory oversight at both the federal and state levels. To the extent the nonprofit is exempt from federal income taxes, it is subject to oversight at the federal level by the IRS. (Depending on the activities of the nonprofit, it might also be subject to other federal government oversight, such as a nonprofit hospital that is subject to U.S. Department of Health and Human Services regulations.)

A nonprofit corporation also is subject to state regulation in the state in which it is incorporated. One important state oversight body is the secretary of state's office, which has filing responsibility of such documents as articles of incorporation, articles of merger, articles of dissolution, and annual or biennial reporting forms. Further, a nonprofit is subject to state regulation in other states where it does business. For a nonprofit that is set up as a charity, the state attorneys general in the states where the nonprofit is incorporated and doing business typically have some type of oversight over the nonprofit corporation. This is especially the case with regard to charitable solicitations, which are subject to the state attorney general's oversight in many states.

DOES IT MAKE SENSE TO SET UP A NEW NONPROFIT? WHAT ARE THE ALTERNATIVES?

Existing Nonprofit

When asked by a client to establish a nonprofit that will have limited resources, it is always helpful to first consider whether there is a better alternative to establishing a new nonprofit. This is due in part to the various statutory and regulatory requirements imposed on nonprofit corporations. In addition, nonprofit corporations must follow specific steps to dissolve. In some states, dissolution requires not only a filing with the appropriate secretary of state office, but also an approval from the state attorney general's office or court.

To the extent there is an existing nonprofit already performing activities or services the client would like to have performed or that could easily incorporate the type of activities desired by the client, it may be advisable to recommend the client consider investigating whether the existing nonprofit would be willing to perform the desired activities. For example, if the client would like to promote a charitable activity and raise funds for such activity, there may be an existing nonprofit that is already involved in promoting similar charitable activities that is willing to work with the client on fundraising activities. By taking this approach, the client could pursue supporting the charitable activity without having to expend resources in incorporating a new nonprofit and obtaining and maintaining its tax-exempt status.

Another popular approach is called "fiscal sponsorship." This approach involves an existing nonprofit (typically a charitable nonprofit corporation) that, as its main purpose, acts as an umbrella entity to a number of projects it "shepherds" as charitable projects. There are two key ways of accomplishing fiscal sponsorship.

The first way is for the project to be a program of the existing entity. The income and expenses are those of the umbrella entity. If anyone is hired for the project, the individual is an employee or contractor of the entity. The project is part of the operations of the entity. Still, it is a discrete project that can include an agreement on roles and responsibilities of the individuals involved in the project.

The second way is to have the umbrella entity accept grant funding, place such funding into a restricted account, and then regrant it to another entity to perform the project. This allows the regranting entity to begin operation without obtaining its own tax-exempt status. A fiscal sponsorship may be attractive to a newly formed nonprofit that must raise money during a start-up phase before it is recognized as tax-exempt by the IRS.

For-Profit Corporation and Limited Liability Company

The concept of social entrepreneurship has become popular in recent years with such purposes accomplished through a for-profit organization, such as a business corporation or limited liability company. Some of the purposes of social entrepreneurship are similar to those of a nonprofit corporation in that the entity is established in whole or in part for a charitable or societal purpose. Still, there are some important distinctions to the extent the entities are formed as for-profit entities. Importantly, unlike the situation with a nonprofit entity, there are owners who can personally benefit from the operations of the entity. This typically is in the form of equity ownership and stock options. It is also possible to have outside investors with these types of entities. It is important to note that such entities generally are not eligible for federal tax-exempt status, so they are not able to receive donations that qualify as deductible contributions under the Internal Revenue Code.[1]

These entities can be in various forms, including business corporations and limited liability companies. Such entities can be owned by individuals, other for-profit entities, or nonprofit corporations.

Low-Profit Limited Liability Company (L3C)

Some states have enacted laws allowing for a variation on LLCs called the low-profit limited liability company (L3C). Most of these types of organizations are for-profit, taxable entities with one or more taxable members who have an ownership interest in the entity. Making a profit typically is a secondary purpose, with the primary purpose being a charitable

1. A limited liability company can be eligible for tax-exempt status under section 501(c)(3) if it meets certain requirements. *See infra* Chapter 3, "Classification of Nonprofits with Tax-Exempt Status under Section 501(c)(3)."

organization. Proponents of the L3C model cite the ability of the entity to be used for permissible program-related investments for private foundations under the Internal Revenue Code.

Benefit Corporation

A number of states have enacted statutes allowing corporations to opt into a legal structure that expressly allows the purpose of the corporation to be expanded beyond advancing the pecuniary interests of its shareholders. Such statutes allow or require directors to consider environmental, societal, or other impacts of corporate activity, even at the expense of shareholder value. Corporations adopting such expanded purposes are commonly referred to as "benefit corporations" or "social purpose corporations."

In some states, the benefit corporation law: (1) requires the corporation consider the general public welfare before acting; (2) permits more specific "public" interests to be considered; and (3) requires the corporation's compliance be measured against a standard imposed by an independent third party. In making decisions, directors are to consider the constituencies relevant to the general public benefit.

In some states, a benefit corporation is required to prepare a "benefit report" to be made available to its shareholders each year. The report is to measure the corporation's benefit performance using a third-party standard. The requirements relating to the third-party standard are very detailed. Some states also have a specific rule for a benefit director who must opine as to the success of the corporation in acting in accordance with its general public purpose and specific public purposes. Some of the statutes authorizing benefit corporations also authorize shareholders to pursue "benefit enforcement proceedings," which are lawsuits over whether a corporation is pursuing or creating the intended general public benefit or specific public benefits.

These corporations are not nonprofit, but continue to be owned by the shareholders. The "benefit" option may be removed or modified by the shareholders at any time and for any reason. They are mentioned here simply because of their growing popularity as a way to achieve certain nonprofit-type purposes without an irrevocable dedication of assets.

Formation of Nonprofit Organizations

2

FORMS OF NONPROFIT ENTITIES

Nonprofit Corporation

The most popular form of nonprofit—and the primary focus of this book—is the nonprofit corporation. It typically is the preferred entity because of the comprehensive statutory structure provided through a state's nonprofit corporation act that usually is similar to the state's for-profit corporation act. Like a for-profit corporation, the nonprofit corporation provides liability protection to its constituents (members of the board of directors, officers, volunteers, and employees) for any debts and liabilities of the corporation. In addition, nonprofit corporations, pursuant to the applicable state nonprofit corporation act, are provided broad powers.

Limited Liability Company

Limited liability companies (LLCs) can be established a nonprofit purpose. Like nonprofit corporations, LLC subject to a comprehensive statutory structure. Still, th fer from nonprofit corporations in some important including the fact that an LLC must have members who have an ownership interest in the LLC. This requirement creates an issue from a tax exemption standpoint because, to date, the IRS has only recognized tax-exempt status for LLCs whose members are tax-exempt.[1]

As discussed in more detail in this book, an LLC may be an attractive form of entity for a nonprofit corporation that is organizing a subsidiary because a single-member LLC is treated as a disregarded entity for federal tax purposes and need not file a separate return with the IRS.[2]

Unincorporated Nonprofit Association

An unincorporated nonprofit association often arises when a group of individuals has embarked on a nonprofit activity but has not incorporated as a nonprofit corporation or other business entity. It often is an informal organization in which the participants may not have addressed legal or organizational issues, including whether to incorporate. Examples include a garden club, a booster club, a local chapter of a state-wide or national association, a union, or a political committee. An unincorporated nonprofit association need not file a document with the secretary of state's office in order to be established.

There can be uncertainty with respect to the rights, duties, and liabilities of the individuals involved with the unincorporated nonprofit association. This has been remedied in recent years in some states by the adoption of an unincorporated nonprofit association act that provides some basic law regarding the operation of an unincorporated nonprofit association.

Some states have adopted the Uniform Law Commission's Revised Uniform Unincorporated Nonprofit Association Act (RUUNAA) or its predecessor, the Uniform Unincorporated Nonprofit Association Act. RUUNAA provides default governance provisions and certain liability protections for members and managers and provides more certainty than

1. *See infra* Chapter 3, "Classification of Nonprofits with Tax-Exempt Status under Section 501(c)(3)."
2. *See infra* Chapter 3, "Classification of Nonprofits with Tax-Exempt Status under Section 501(c)(3), Limited Liability Companies."

the common law for a limited number of legal problems. RUUNAA is intended to provide a limited set of rules and protections for small nonprofit organizations that have not chosen to elect as a nonprofit corporation.

As the activities of an unincorporated nonprofit association increase, consideration may be given to incorporating as a nonprofit corporation. Still, it may make sense in limited situations to continue the activity as an unincorporated nonprofit association such as where its activities will not present significant risk to the organization or the individuals involved.

The IRS will recognize an unincorporated nonprofit association as a tax-exempt entity, as will most state regulators, if it is sufficiently organized to operate under a set of written governing documents, typically bylaws.

Charitable Trust

The most common form of a nonprofit is a nonprofit corporation. This has not always been the case. In the early days of the United States, nonprofits were more often established in the form of trusts, most commonly charitable trusts. This came from the Statute of Charitable Uses adopted in England in 1601, which allowed trusts to be formed for charitable purposes. Charitable trusts can operate like nonprofit corporations.

Formation of a charitable trust does not require any filing with the secretary of state's office, but a trust instrument still is required. The trust is formed for purposes of benefiting a nonprofit purpose. The trust has trustees who are responsible for the operation of the trust. Trustees are held to a higher fiduciary standard than corporate directors, and the default form of trustee decision-making is different, usually requiring unanimous consent.

TYPES OF NONPROFIT CORPORATIONS

Once it has been determined that the attorney is working with a nonprofit corporation, it is important to determine the type of nonprofit corporation: a public benefit corporation, mutual benefit corporation, or religious corporation.

Some states, such as California, recognize the differences among these types of nonprofit corporations in their statutes. Others do not expressly recognize such classifications. Regardless of whether the applicable nonprofit corporation act uses such classifications, it is helpful to think about the type of nonprofit corporation in these terms because the rules imposed by the applicable state nonprofit corporation act for each type can differ.

Public Benefit Corporation

Most nonprofits are public benefit corporations (also called "charitable corporations").[3] These entities normally will qualify for tax-exempt status under Internal Revenue Code section 501(c)(3) or 501(c)(4) as charitable or social-welfare organizations. Examples of the types of entities that fall into this category include libraries, museums, hospitals, and schools. Oftentimes, a public benefit corporation provides a service or product to the public that generally is not offered by a for-profit enterprise. The nonprofit may have a membership, but many public benefit corporations do not have members because most state nonprofit corporation laws allow nonprofits to be governed by only a board of directors without members. The activities of this type of nonprofit typically are available to the public in general.

Mutual Benefit Corporation

A mutual benefit corporation is formed primarily to serve the members of the nonprofit corporation as opposed to the general public. Many of the attributes of a mutual benefit corporation are similar to those of a for-profit entity, and in some ways the members of a mutual benefit corporation look more like shareholders with regard to certain governance rights. Still, an important distinction is that members of a mutual benefit corporation do not have the right of distribution from the corporation. Examples of mutual benefit corporations include homeowner associations, chambers of commerce, trade associations (such as state bar associations and the American Bar Association), fraternal organizations, veterans organizations, and country clubs and other social clubs. Many mutual benefit corporations establish their tax-exempt status under section 501(c)(6) or 501(c)(7).

---

3. A nonprofit "public benefit corporation" is not to be confused with a Delaware "public benefit corporation," which is a type of for-profit benefit corporation.

Religious Corporation

A religious corporation is similar to a public benefit corporation but is set up for religious purposes. For constitutional and policy reasons, however, nonprofit corporation acts will provide religious corporations with more flexibility in structure and operations than public benefit corporations.

Other Types of Nonprofit Corporations

Some states have additional categories of nonprofit corporations such as consumer cooperatives.

ORGANIZATIONAL DOCUMENTS

Organizational documents differ depending on the type of nonprofit organization created. With a nonprofit corporation, it is necessary to have articles of incorporation, typically filed with the state's secretary of state office, and bylaws. With a charitable trust, it is necessary to have a trust instrument or other document that defines the type of entity and how it functions. A limited liability company has articles of organization or a certificate of organization, typically filed with the secretary of state, and an operating agreement. For an unincorporated association, it is helpful to have a written document, often in the form of bylaws or other form of governance agreement.[4]

Nonprofit Corporation—Articles of Incorporation

In order to create a nonprofit corporation, it is necessary to file articles of incorporation with the state secretary of state's office together with the applicable filing fee. Such document establishes the existence of the nonprofit corporation. Some provisions of the articles are similar to for-profit corporation articles of corporation, whereas other provisions are unique to nonprofit corporations.

4. RUUNAA contemplates the unincorporated nonprofit association will have "governing principles" in the form of an agreement between the members that governs the purpose and operation of the association and the rights and obligations of its members and managers.

Mandatory Provisions

The provisions contained in articles of incorporation will vary depending upon the state of incorporation in accordance with the requirements imposed by the state nonprofit corporation law. As a result, reference to the state nonprofit corporation act is essential in preparing the articles.

Some common mandatory requirements include the following:

- **Name.** A nonprofit corporation must have a name that is distinguishable from other legal organizations incorporated in the same state. In many states, a nonprofit corporation is not required to include in its name the word "corporation," "incorporated," "company," "limited," or any abbreviations thereof.
- **Purpose Clause.** This is an important part of the articles of incorporation. If the nonprofit is to have tax-exempt status under Internal Revenue Code section 501(c)(3), the articles of incorporation must limit the purposes of the nonprofit to one or more exempt purposes permitted under section 501(c)(3). A state nonprofit corporation act may impose other requirements on what must be stated with regard to the purposes of the nonprofit.
- **Irrevocable Dedication of Assets.** If the nonprofit is to have tax-exempt status under section 501(c)(3), it is necessary to include a provision that prohibits the assets of the corporation from being used to benefit an individual, and instead to use them for the charitable purposes of the corporation. It also is necessary to include a provision that identifies the disposition of the assets upon dissolution of the entity to ensure that the assets will be used for a charitable purpose even after the corporation ceases to operate.[5] Nonprofits seeking other forms of exempt status generally must demonstrate only noninurement of benefits to the

5. For mandatory provisions for organizations organized exclusively for one or more section 501(c)(3) purposes, *see* 26 C.F.R. §§ 1.501(c)(3)-1(b)(1)(i) and 1.501(a)(3)-1(b)(1)(iv)(4). I.R.S. Publication 557, Tax-Exempt Status for Your Organization, contains samples of language that will meet the organizational test.

members and managers, with the possible exception of liquidating distributions.

- **Registered Agent.** It is necessary to include a provision that identifies the registered agent for service of process along with the address of the registered agent. A nonprofit corporation always must have a registered agent in place. For some nonprofits, the registered agent will be a volunteer of the organization. It is important to ensure that a replacement registered agent is substituted in the event this volunteer ceases to be involved with the organization. A nonprofit corporation can be administratively dissolved for failure to file its annual or biennial report, which typically is sent to the registered agent. If the volunteer is no longer involved in the organization, it is possible that the report will not be submitted, and an administrative dissolution will occur.
- **Incorporator.** It often is necessary to include the name and address of one or more incorporators of the nonprofit corporation. The role of incorporator is similar to that in a for-profit corporation. The individual is responsible for signing and filing the articles of incorporation and convening an organizational meeting or otherwise getting the first board of directors appointed unless the initial board of directors is identified in the articles of incorporation.
- **Other State Requirements.** There may be other types of information required to be included in the articles of incorporation. For instance, in California and states that have adopted the ABA Revised Model Nonprofit Corporation Act, it is necessary to identify the type of nonprofit (i.e., public benefit, mutual benefit, or religious). In states that have adopted the ABA Model Nonprofit Corporation Act, Third Edition (MNCA) (which replaced the Revised Model Nonprofit Corporation Act), it is necessary to describe any "designated body" that has been assigned powers that otherwise rest with the board of directors. In addition, some states require that the nonprofit identify in the articles of incorporation whether it has any members.

Optional Provisions

State nonprofit corporation acts often allow for the inclusion of permissible provisions. In terms of the nonmandatory provisions in the articles of incorporation, the following may be included:

- **Initial Board of Directors.** The names and addresses of the initial members of the board of directors can be identified in the articles of incorporation. The inclusion of this type of information can be helpful as it allows the board to convene the organizational meeting (as opposed to the incorporator). Some nonprofits desire to minimize public information on the members of the board of directors. As a result, they may opt not to identify the board members in the articles of incorporation (because it is publicly available from the state secretary of state's office). Still, states often will require annual or biennial reports to be filed with the secretary of state's office that identify one or more of the directors of the nonprofit. Such documents are also public record. Further, this information will be furnished when the organization files for its exempt status. Another reason not to identify the directors in the articles of incorporation is that, unless eliminated by future amendments, their names will remain in the articles long after they have ceased serving as directors.
- **Elimination/Limitation of Liability of Directors.** In some states, including those that have adopted the MNCA, a provision may be included in the articles of incorporation that eliminates or limits the liability of a director to the corporation or its members for money damages.[6]
- **Indemnification.** Similarly, some states, including those that have adopted the MNCA, allow for the most expansive indemnification rights only if a provision is included in the articles of incorporation.

6. The MNCA provides an "automatic" liability shield for directors of a charitable corporation. MNCA § 8.31(d). For directors of a noncharitable nonprofit corporation, the articles of incorporation must include the liability shield language in order for directors to be protected from liability to the nonprofit and its members. MNCA § 2.02(c).

- **Management of Nonprofit.** It is possible to include provisions in the articles of incorporation addressing the management and regulation of the nonprofit corporation.
- **Defining, Limiting, and Regulating Powers.** A provision can be included in the articles of incorporation that describes the powers and limitations of the corporation, its board of directors, members, and any class of members.
- **Membership Differences.** A provision can be included that describes the characteristics, qualifications, rights, limitations, and obligations for each class of members. The management of the nonprofit; the description of any powers and limitations of the corporation, its board of directors, members, and any class of members; and any membership differences also can be addressed in the bylaws, which may be a more proper document to address these topics.
- **Amendments to Articles of Incorporation.** A provision can be included that describes the process under which the articles of incorporation may be amended. In multi-level organizations and organizations with an outside sponsor, it is common to include a provision in the articles of incorporation requiring approval of the superior organization or sponsor of any amendments to the articles of incorporation or bylaws.
- **Religious Organizations.** Religious organizations may have fidelity clauses to a particular creed or denomination.

From a drafting standpoint, it often is best to include only those provisions that are mandatory and those permissive provisions that may provide additional protection to the nonprofit or its directors and officers and cannot be included in the bylaws. A main reason for such recommendation is that the articles of incorporation is a public document that requires amendments to be filed with the secretary of state's office, whereas the bylaws—a document typically referenced more frequently by an organization and its directors and officers—can be amended without a filing with the secretary of state's office. Another reason is that articles of incorporation typically are harder to amend than bylaws. In order to avoid unnecessary conflict, it is best not to cover the same subject matter in both the articles of incorporation and bylaws. Of the permissive provisions listed, however, a nonprofit always should consider including in the articles of incorporation those permitted under state law to limit liability of the directors and provide maximum indemnification protection to the directors and officers.

Nonprofit Corporation—Bylaws

The bylaws are a governance document of the organization that is not filed with any secretary of state's office. Depending on the state of incorporation, however, they may need to be provided to the state attorney general. They also may need to be included in an exemption application filed with the IRS depending on the exemption form used.

The bylaws contain a description of the basic powers, rights, duties, and limitations of the members (if there are members), the board of directors, and the officers. To the extent the nonprofit corporation has members, the bylaws often is the document used to describe important aspects of membership.

The bylaws are important to the governance of the organization for two reasons. First, the bylaws set forth the rules of governance of the organization, including the steps required for member action and board of director action to be effective. Second, many nonprofit corporation acts contain "default" provisions that will control unless different terms are set in the articles of incorporation or bylaws. As a result, to the extent the organization would like to be subject to rules that differ from the default rules, it is important to address those rules in the bylaws. Given this importance, the attorney must give careful attention to those documents. To the extent there are inconsistent provisions in the articles of incorporation and bylaws that overlap, the provisions in the articles of incorporation will control.

Some organizations, particularly older ones, have both a constitution and bylaws as separate documents. This is somewhat more common in unincorporated associations. In that case, the constitution contains the more important provisions not included in the articles of incorporation and should be harder to amend than the bylaws. In general, the more modern thinking is to have one combined document. Regardless of what they are called, and whether they rest in one document or two documents, they are "bylaws" under most states' nonprofit corporation laws.

Sources to Consider When Drafting Bylaws

For guidance on preparing or reviewing bylaws, helpful resources include:

- applicable state nonprofit corporation act;
- applicable state charitable solicitation laws;
- the Internal Revenue Code;
- sector-specific legal requirements, e.g., a federally qualified health center is required under federal regulation to have a certain minimum number of board members, which would be addressed in the bylaws; and
- state liability shields/volunteer limitation of liability laws.

Subject Areas Covered in Bylaws

Members

As discussed above, nonprofit corporations may have members, but in most states they also may forgo members.[7] In addition, the concept of "member" and the rights of a member will differ among nonprofit corporations. State nonprofit corporation acts typically treat an individual or entity that has the ability to elect one or more directors or has other voting power with regard to significant matters as a "member" under the act. This is important because the act often will provide certain rights to members.

Some kinds of nonprofit organizations, such as those associated with performing arts, public interests, or the needs of special or vulnerable populations, often have a group of individuals and/or entities that are referred to as "members" that do not have the ability to elect directors or vote on other significant matters. They may have member benefits relating to nonprofit organization's activities, such as special access to discounts in admissions, tickets, or promotional items. Without such voting rights, they typically are not considered "members" under a nonprofit corporation act. A nonprofit might have "special access"-type members as a means to recognize donors or derive revenue by creating a sustainable group of individuals

---

7. This is not the case in Delaware where members are required for all nonprofit corporations.

or others who support participation in the organization's mission. In such circumstances, these members often will have only those rights that are set out in the articles of incorporation and bylaws with no reference to the applicable state nonprofit corporation act. The bylaws should make clear that these "members" have no voting rights.

Many states recognize delegate assemblies as an intermediate body between the members and board of directors. For such organizations, the members may have only the right to elect delegates who, in turn, elect directors. If that is the case, the bylaws must be drafted carefully to ensure that the individual members do not inadvertently retain statutory rights of members.

When a nonprofit corporation has "members," it is important to set forth in the bylaws various member-related provisions. The following terms are especially important if the corporation has members with voting rights, but some provisions also are useful with a nonvoting membership. These include the following:

- **Qualification/Selection.** The bylaws should address how an individual or entity becomes a member of the nonprofit corporation. This may involve reference to another document, such as a membership application or policy document, but there should be some criteria for determining membership.
- **Classes of Members.** To the extent the organization will have more than one class of membership, the bylaws should provide a description of the different classes of membership and their respective rights, qualifications, and expectations.
- **Dues.** In the event there are dues requirements imposed on members, a general reference to this point should be included. Under many nonprofit corporation acts, the liability of a member to pay dues continues even after the individual or entity is no longer a member with regard to dues owed prior to termination of the membership. Some nonprofits find it helpful to include a provision in the bylaws making this point clear in order to avoid a dispute with a former member who has unpaid dues.
- **Member Representatives.** For nonprofit corporations that allow for members that are entities (as opposed to individuals), the bylaws should include a provision addressing the process for

a member to designate a representative to act on the member's behalf in the governance of the organization.

- **Termination/Suspension.** State nonprofit corporation acts often recognize the ability of a nonprofit corporation to terminate or suspend a member, and some of these acts include procedures for such action. The bylaws should include a description of the general grounds for termination and suspension as well as the process for such action. Otherwise, the organization may lack any clear way to remove members. In addition, if a person remains on the membership list after ceasing any involvement in the organization, it may be difficult to meet the quorum requirements.
- **Resignation.** A description of how a member may resign from the nonprofit corporation can be helpful to avoid any confusion if there is ever a desire for a member to cease to be part of the organization.
- **Reinstatement.** Nonprofit corporations often will permit the reinstatement of a member who meets certain requirements. The reinstatement criteria and process can be addressed in the bylaws or in another document approved by the board.
- **Membership Transfers.** In some states, it is possible for members in certain types of nonprofits, such as mutual benefit corporations (e.g., country clubs), to sell their membership back to the nonprofit corporation or to transfer their membership to another individual or entity. To the extent this type of transfer is permissible (and the nonprofit wants to allow for transfers), a provision can be included in the bylaws to address the process.
- **Annual/Regular/Special Meetings.** Especially with members that elect directors or vote on other important matters, it is important to have provisions in the bylaws that address how members take action. The primary means for taking action is through annual, regular, or special meetings of the members. The bylaws should address how annual, regular, and special meetings may be called.
- **Written Consents and Ballot Voting.** Many state nonprofit corporation acts permit members to take action by written consent and/or ballot voting instead of holding an annual, regular, or special meeting. Some states and the MNCA permit such action to

be taken with less than unanimous consent/vote.[8] To the extent the nonprofit corporation desires to allow for member consents or ballot voting, the bylaws can set forth the procedure for obtaining consents and/or ballots, and the minimum vote that is necessary for action to be deemed taken by the members. In many states, electronic consents and ballots are permissible, which can be addressed in the bylaws.

- **Proxies.** Many state nonprofit acts include default provisions allowing members to vote by proxy. Few membership organizations actually use proxies on a regular basis. If the organization does not want to permit the use of proxies, the bylaws should clearly prohibit them. If proxies are permissible, it is recommended the board of directors adopt a policy on recognition of proxies.
- **Notices to Members.** The bylaws should address the requirements for notice to members about meetings. Many state nonprofit corporation acts permit electronic notices (which might be accomplished via e-mail) if certain conditions are met. Publication of notice also may be permissible in the organization's regular membership magazine or newsletter.
- **Waiver of Notices.** The process for allowing members to waive any required notices should be addressed in the bylaws.
- **Quorum.** The bylaws should include a requirement on the minimum requirements necessary to have a quorum for a meeting of the members. State nonprofit corporation acts often provide a great deal of flexibility to the organization in determining satisfactory quorum. As a result, in some states, the quorum can be very low, such as the number of the members that show up for a meeting. This can be beneficial for nonprofits with large memberships that find it difficult to have members attend meetings; however, it also can give power to a small group of people who show up for the member meetings. As a result, careful consideration must be given to determining the appropriate number of members for quorum purposes.

8. *See, e.g.*, MNCA § 7.04.

- **Voting Rights.** It is important for bylaws to address any difference in voting rights among members if a difference exists. Otherwise, the general rule is that there is one vote per member. Some nonprofit corporation acts permit cumulative voting. If a nonprofit corporation is to allow for cumulative voting, it is important to include a provision in the articles of incorporation or bylaws.
- **Conduct of Meetings.** The general procedural rules for holding a meeting can be a helpful provision included in the bylaws in order to avoid a dispute that may arise during a meeting. There are no prescribed rules with regard to how a meeting is to be held; as a result, a nonprofit can have a great deal of flexibility in determining the actual rules for the meeting. Typically, it is not a good idea to include extensive procedural rules in bylaws. It usually is better, as such rules are needed, to authorize the members or the board to approve rules of order. In organizations with large membership meetings or delegate assemblies with significant power, it might be useful to adopt a meeting guide (sometimes called a parliamentary authority) in the bylaws.
- **Fundamental Transactions.** In many states, the bylaws may contain provisions establishing higher than normal voting requirements for fundamental transactions (e.g., amendments to articles of incorporation and bylaws, mergers, sale of assets, and dissolutions) than the statutory minimums.

Election or Appointment of Directors

To the extent there are members with voting rights, the directors often are elected by such members. Many state nonprofit corporation acts are flexible, however, and can allow directors to be elected or appointed by members, delegates, the directors themselves, some other party, or a combination of the foregoing.

- **Members.** The most common means for election of directors in a membership organization is through a vote of the members. To the extent there is a large membership, the election of directors may present challenges for the nonprofit corporation due to difficulties in managing membership meetings and votes. As a result, ballot voting by mail or electronic transmission can be an important consideration.

- **Delegates.** Delegates may be part of the governance of a nonprofit corporation where there is a large membership and it is necessary to centralize the governance of the organization (or director election) to a smaller group of individuals. Large religious organizations and trade organizations often use delegates. For these organizations, the bylaws frequently allow a delegate assembly to elect directors and set broad policy directives for the organization.
- **Directors.** A common form of election is where the directors elect their successors. In some states, this type of an election can take place even when there are members. One justification for having directors elect their successors is that the directors are likely to be the most knowledgeable with regard to the operations and needs of the organization (as compared to the members who may be less engaged with the organization). A drawback to allowing the directors to elect their successors is that the power is limited to a narrow group of people. A board that is elected in this manner is sometimes called a "self-perpetuating" board.[9]
- ***Ex Officio.*** An individual may automatically be deemed a member of the board of directors by virtue of the position the individual holds within the nonprofit corporation or elsewhere.[10] For example, it is possible that the president or chief executive officer, an employee of the organization, might automatically be a member of the board of directors. Unless otherwise specified in the bylaws, *ex officio* directors have the same rights to vote as any other director. If the bylaws define someone as an "*ex officio* nonvoting director," that person should not be counted for quorum purposes.

---

9. In cases where there is a self-perpetuating board, it often is helpful to have a nominating committee charged with seeking out new board members with diverse viewpoints and experiences.
10. Sometimes, outsiders are *ex officio* members. For example, the president of a college might, by virtue of the position, serve as a member of the board of the alumni association.

- **Appointment by Third Parties.** A nonprofit corporation can provide in its bylaws that one or more directors are elected or appointed by a third party that may not otherwise have a role in the governance of the organization. For example, a nonprofit established to benefit a city may give the right to appoint a director to a city representative.

Board of Directors

An important part of the bylaws is the description of the powers and duties of the board of directors of the nonprofit corporation. The areas that should be covered in the bylaws include the following:

- **Selection.** The manner in which the members of the board of directors is elected or appointed should be set forth in the bylaws. As described above, nonprofit corporations typically have a great deal of flexibility in who will be involved in electing or appointing the directors.
- **Types of Directors.** State nonprofit corporation acts generally contemplate one class of directors, all of whom have certain duties (including the duty of care and the duty of loyalty) and rights—primarily in the form of a voting on matters. As noted above, it is possible an individual may be a director by virtue of that person's position in the corporation itself or in another organization. This is often referred to as an "*ex officio*" director. To the extent the bylaws provide for an *ex officio* director, it is important to expressly state whether such individual has voting rights. As indicated above, if silent on issue, the *ex officio* director has the same voting rights as other directors.

  Some nonprofits desire to have classes of persons they refer to as directors who do not have all of the rights of "regular" directors. This may include former directors who the nonprofit corporation would like to have stay engaged with the organization. Some titles used for these individuals include "honorary directors" and "advisory directors." Given the legal responsibilities imposed on regular directors, and in order to avoid any confusion, it is recommended nonprofits avoid the use of a "director" title to refer to these individuals. Regardless of whether the person is called a "director," it is important to make clear in the bylaws the rights and responsibilities of these individuals.[11]

- **Number.** The bylaws should set forth the specific number of directors. Alternatively, many state nonprofit corporation acts permit a nonprofit to identify a range of the number of directors who might serve at any given time with the exact number to be set by the board or otherwise.
- **Tenure/Terms.** In general, director terms can be one year or multiple years. It is important to identify the length of the terms in the bylaws. For a larger board of directors, consideration should be given to permitting staggered terms. A main benefit of staggered terms is continuity. A corporation opting to have staggered terms typically will divide the total number of directors into groups. For example, a board of 15 directors might divide the directors into three groups (generally equal in number), with one group elected each year for a term of three years. Unlike the situation with for-profit corporations, which generally are required to identify staggered terms in the articles of incorporation, a nonprofit corporation often may provide for staggered terms in the bylaws. Some nonprofits provide for a set term of years that cannot be exceeded without at least a one-year gap in service. Term limits can be helpful for a variety of reasons including addressing attendance problems and ensuring that the board has engaged members and is not dominated by one of two people. Term limits, if desired, should be clearly provided in the bylaws.
- **Qualifications.** The minimum qualifications (if any) of the directors should be described in the bylaws. In a membership organization, the bylaws often require that a director be a member.
- **Resignation and Removal.** The bylaws should set forth the rules relating to the resignation and removal of directors. Resignation typically may occur with written notice to the president or

11. Some states authorize "alternative directors" when the elected or appointed directors cannot attend meetings. This may be useful for representative boards where some directors are appointed by third parties.

secretary of the nonprofit corporation. Removal normally can be effected through the same means by which the director was elected, i.e., if the members elected the director, the members may remove the director. Some state nonprofit corporation acts permit the board of directors to remove a director regardless of who elected or appointed the director.

- **Regular/Special Meetings/Notices.** The bylaws should address how regular and special meetings are called and the notice requirements. To the extent the nonprofit corporation contemplates electronic meetings, such as meetings held via conference call, it is important to note such permissibility in the bylaws.
- **Order of Business.** It is important for the bylaws to describe how the order of business of the board of directors meetings will be handled. Although some nonprofits will utilize formal rules, such as the special board rules in Robert's Rules of Order, such rules are not statutorily required. In addition, for most nonprofits, formal rules may prove to be too cumbersome because they do not have large deliberative bodies. The bylaws can identify some simple rules of procedure or empower the board or an officer (such as the chair) to determine the rules.
- **Quorum.** It is important to describe the quorum necessary to hold a director meeting and to allow voting. It is common for state nonprofit corporation acts to provide that the "default" quorum is a majority of the directors. Such acts generally restrict nonprofit corporations from having a quorum that is less than one-third of all directors.
- **Voting.** The required number of votes necessary for board action to be deemed taken should be described in the bylaws. To the extent the bylaws are silent, the "default" provision in the state nonprofit corporation act—which typically is majority vote of those present—will govern. This means that abstentions at a board meeting count as "no votes." Some nonprofits find it important to impose a greater-than-majority vote on some matters. This often is called a "supermajority" vote. If desired, it would be important to identify in the bylaws the matters requiring such a vote and the minimum number of votes to meet such a "supermajority" requirement.

- **Written Consent of Directors.** Many nonprofit corporation acts permit directors to take action via written consent in lieu of holding a meeting. Such consents typically must be signed by all of the voting directors in order to be effective. There are a few states that allow for consents or e-mail voting to be something less than unanimous. As a result, it is important to check the applicable nonprofit corporation act.
- **Electronic Communications/Action.** Most nonprofit corporation acts permit electronic notices as well as electronic action (via written consent). A provision in the bylaws expressly permitting this type of communication can be helpful.
- **No Proxies.** Sometimes nonprofit corporations want to permit directors to submit proxies for votes to occur at the board of directors meeting. Although proxies may be permissible at the member level, they are not permissible for board action in many states.
- **Compensation.** Although most nonprofits do not compensate their directors, it generally is permissible to provide reasonable compensation for board service. To the extent a director is to receive compensation, it is advisable to include a provision in the bylaws that permits such compensation.
- **Committees.** Board committees can be important to the governance of the nonprofit corporation. These committees, with certain limited exceptions, can be a delegated board authority or serve in an advisory capacity. Many nonprofits will include detailed descriptions of the standing board committees (and their responsibilities) in the bylaws. A drawback to having a detailed description is the likelihood that the committees end up not complying with the bylaw requirements because they develop their own process for operation over time. As a result, sometimes a less-is-more approach with regard to committee descriptions may be better. Bylaws can include a more general or "big picture" description about the rights and duties of the board to create committees. Many nonprofit organizations use board resolutions, committee charters, or other documents that describe the specific duties of each committee, rather than provide a detailed description (or even the names) of all committees. To the extent any such committees are delegated review or approval powers that would

otherwise be the responsibility of the board, the board should adopt and revise, from time to time as appropriate, such charter or similar document. This type of document should be easier to change over time than the bylaws. It is important to review state law on composition and permitted activities of committees. Committees with power to act in place of the board generally must consist entirely of board members whereas advisory committees can be made up of non-board members.

Officers

Whereas the board of directors is given authority to set policies and determine the general direction of the nonprofit corporation, the officers are expected to implement the decisions of the board of directors and oversee the day-to-day activities of the nonprofit corporation. State laws vary on specific requirements to have a particular "named" officer. Most organizations typically have, at a minimum, a president and/or chair, secretary, and treasurer. The officers of the nonprofit should be described in the bylaws along with their rights and responsibilities.

In addition, the bylaws should describe how officers are selected. In most cases, the board of directors selects the officers; however, in some nonprofit organizations, the membership select the officers. It is important to clarify whether officers are volunteers (often with set terms) or employees (who typically serve at the pleasure of the board, subject to an employment contract).

Other Subject Areas

Other common subject areas addressed in bylaws include the following:

- **Receipt and Disbursement of Funds.** A bylaw provision describing the officers and other representatives in the nonprofit corporation with the authority to receive and disburse funds is important for helping establish such authority to third parties (such as banks and other lending institutions) that are conducting business with the nonprofit corporation.
- **Corporate Records and Reports.** State nonprofit corporation acts often provide rights to members and directors to have access

to certain corporate records. The bylaws can set forth these rights and must do so if it wishes to modify the rights (to the extent permissible under state law).

- **Amendment of Bylaws.** The process for amending the bylaws should be addressed in the bylaws. Otherwise, the amendment process will "default" to the state nonprofit corporation act.

Policies, Board Resolutions, and Charters

Other important board governance documents include policies, charters, and board of director resolutions. Various governance policies are discussed in more detail in Chapter 4, *Governance Matters*, Board Policies. The board of directors might pass a "standing" resolution that addresses areas that are not specified in the bylaws. An example is a resolution setting forth by dollar thresholds the authority of officers to make binding commitments on behalf of the organization. In addition, as discussed above with regard to committees, charters can describe various aspects of committees, such as their purposes and authority, which are not set forth in the bylaws. All of these documents generally are changed more frequently than bylaws, and by having them separate from the bylaws, it is not necessary to comply with the bylaws' amendment requirements to make changes.

Organizational Meeting/Written Consent

Upon incorporation of a nonprofit corporation, it is necessary for the organization to take certain organizational steps. This can be accomplished through an organizational meeting called by the incorporator or the initial board of directors if an initial board of directors is identified in the articles of incorporation. The organizational meeting also can be accomplished through a written consent of the incorporator and/or initial board of directors. The meeting/consent should cover the following:

- election of board of directors and officers;
- adoption of the bylaws of the corporation;
- appointment of any committees;

- approval of establishment of any checking or bank accounts;
- approval or authorization to proceed with the filing of an application for tax-exempt status;
- adoption of a corporate seal (if any);
- designation of the accounting year (if not identified in the bylaws);
- approval of payment of incorporation expenses;
- continuing authorization for state informational filings and state and federal tax filings;
- designation of principal office location;
- approval of filing of any applications for necessary licensure;
- approval of acquisition of insurance;
- adoption of policies; and
- release of incorporator from any further duties and liabilities.

If the incorporator is involved with the organizational meeting, the incorporator generally elects the directors, and then the directors proceed with approving the other organizational items.

Tax Issues for Nonprofit Corporations

3

COMMON TYPES OF TAX EXEMPTIONS UNDER INTERNAL REVENUE CODE

The Internal Revenue Code (IRC) recognizes 29 different types of tax-exempts entities under section 501(c).[1] In addition, there are other types of tax-exempt entities described in sections 501, 521, and 527. The attributes, benefits, and obligations of tax exemption depend on the particular tax-exempt status of the entity. Below is a summary of the four most common types of tax-exempt entities. The summary highlights only the most common issues applicable to certain tax-exempt entities and does not provide a detailed analysis of such issues. The IRS website has a great deal of tax information useful to nonprofits and their attorneys.[2]

1. Appendix B sets forth the specific classifications under section 501(c).
2. *See Tax Information for Charities & Other Nonprofits* (www.irs.gov/charities-non-profit).

Section 501(c)(3)—Charity

The most common type of federal tax exemption is under section 501(c)(3). It is the charitable exemption that often is the most difficult to obtain. The section 501(c)(3) charity generally is the only type of tax-exempt entity that is able to receive tax-deductible charitable contributions under section 170, which can be a key benefit to donors. It must be operated for charitable, religious, educational, scientific, and/or similar purposes. The organization must be organized for the benefit of the public or as a religious corporation. A mutual benefit corporation, such as a trade association or country club, does not typically qualify for tax-exempt status under section 501(c)(3).

In order for a nonprofit corporation to qualify for tax-exempt status under section 501(c)(3), it must operate within the following parameters set forth in that section, and as amended from time to time by Congress:

- organized exclusively for a permissible exempt purpose;
- operated exclusively for exempt purposes;
- no net earnings or assets of the organization may inure to the benefit of any private person;
- no involvement in political campaign activity, either supporting or opposing candidates for public office; and
- no involvement in substantial legislative lobbying.

The last of two of these requirements are discussed in more detail below.[3]

Some common red flags or problems that arise for nonprofit corporations seeking exemption from federal taxation under section 501(c)(3) include the following:

- the "purposes" description in the articles of incorporation is too broad and not restricted to those purposes permissible under section 501(c)(3);
- the size of the charitable class is too small;

3. *See infra* Chapter 3, "Prohibition on Involvement in Political Campaigns and Limits on Legislative Lobbying."

- the organization engages in social activities that serve a noncharitable class or classes;
- the organization primarily engages in fundraising, but lacks charitable operations or qualified "supporting organization" status discussed at Chapter 3, *Tax Issues for Nonprofit Corporations*, Classifications of Nonprofits Tax-Exempt Under Section 501 (c)(3);
- the organization engages in commercial activities that compete with for-profit counterparts; and
- the actual purpose of the nonprofit is to enrich/benefit insiders.

Charitable Contributions

There are various requirements with regard to tax deductible contributions to organizations that have tax-exempt status under section 501(c)(3). Generally, it is possible to deduct contributions of money or property that are made to, or for the use of, such an organization. If the contributor receives or expects to receive a financial or economic benefit as a result of making the contribution, the contributor cannot deduct that part of the contribution that represents the value of benefit to be received. There are substantiation and record-keeping rules imposed on donors who intend to claim a charitable contribution deduction. A donor cannot claim a tax deduction for any cash, check or other monetary contribution unless the donor maintains a record of such contribution. A donor cannot claim a tax deduction for any single contribution of $250 or more unless the donor obtains a contemporaneous written acknowledgment of the contribution from the recipient public charity.[4]

Section 501(c)(4)—Social Welfare

A nonprofit corporation that qualifies for tax-exempt status under section 501(c)(4) is set up to further a social welfare purpose, which is defined more broadly than the charitable purposes of a nonprofit that

---

4. For more details on requirements relating to charitable contributions, *see* I.R.S. Publication 1771, *Charitable Contributions – Substantiation and Disclosure Requirements*; I.R.S. Publication 526, *Charitable Contributions*.

qualifies for tax-exempt status under section 501(c)(3). Types of entities falling within this category include organizations focusing on civil rights, poverty, and environmental protection. These often are called "advocacy groups."

To qualify for an exemption under section 501(c)(4), it is necessary that the organization's net earnings must be devoted primarily to charitable, educational, or recreational purposes. In addition, no part of the organization's net earnings can inure to the benefit of any private shareholder or individual. Contributions to a section 501(c)(4) organization do not qualify for tax deductions under section 170. The organization should notify prospective donors that their contributions are not deductible as charitable contributions.

Because a section 501(c)(4) organization is not eligible to receive tax-deductible charitable contributions, it typically is easier to meet the requirements under this section than under section 501(c)(3). This type of entity is also subject to fewer restrictions than an entity with tax-exempt status under section 501(c)(3). For example, this type of entity is able to engage in more lobbying activities as well as electioneering activities.

A nonprofit with tax-exempt status under section 501(c)(4) is sometimes referred to being "501(c)(3) light" because its attributes are similar to those of an entity with tax-exempt status under section 501(c)(3). Like a nonprofit with tax-exempt status under section 501(c)(3), this type of entity typically is a nonprofit corporation organized for the benefit of the public.

Section 501(c)(6)—Trade/Professional Associations

Trade and professional organizations can qualify for tax-exempt status under section 501(c)(6). These types of entities typically are mutual benefit corporations with a membership base that promotes the common business interests of members in a particular line of business. These organizations serve the membership through services, advertising campaigns, lobbying activities, and/or conferences and other events to promote the members' common business interests. For such organizations, no part of the net earnings may inure to the benefit of any individual and the organizations cannot be organized for profit or organized to engage in any activity ordinarily carried on for profit.

Section 501(c)(7)—Social Clubs

Social clubs, such as country clubs, athletic clubs, and garden clubs, are able to qualify as tax-exempt under section 501(c)(7). Only certain types of section 501(c)(7) organizations' income are exempt from federal income tax, so they do not enjoy as favorable treatment (in terms of exemption from federal income taxes) as do other tax-exempt entities. No part of such an organization's net earnings can inure to the benefit of any person having a personal or private interest in the activities of the organization.

STATE TAX EXEMPTION

The mere fact an entity qualifies for federal tax-exempt status under the IRC does not automatically mean the entity is exempt from income tax under state law. In some states, such as California, it is also necessary to separately apply for and obtain exemption from state taxing authorities. In other states, there will be an automatic exemption based on federal income tax exemption status. Organizations that are exempt from federal income tax exemption may, but do not always, qualify for exemption from other state and local taxes, such as property and sales taxes.

CLASSIFICATIONS OF NONPROFITS TAX-EXEMPT UNDER SECTION 501(C)(3)

Within the section 501(c)(3) classification, there are two overarching categories: public charities and private foundations. As part of the application process, a nonprofit, if it has a choice, typically will attempt to qualify as a public charity. If the nonprofit is not able to qualify for public charity status, it will default to private foundation status.

Private Foundations

Private foundations generally are funded by one large donor, such as a for-profit organization, or a few large donors. Due to concerns about having a nonprofit unduly benefit its large funders, organizations with such status are subject to more restrictions than a public charity. These include:

- a self-dealing prohibition that prohibits certain financial transactions between the private foundation and the donor organization or individuals;

- stricter rules addressing distributions, including minimum distribution requirements;
- more restricted grant-making;
- limitations on investments in for-profit subsidiaries of private foundations and on other "jeopardizing investments";
- greater limitations on the deductibility of a donor's charitable contributions to private foundations than for public charities; and
- excise tax on net investment income.

Attorneys involved with private foundation issues should familiarize themselves with these detailed rules, which are beyond the scope of this book.[5]

Public Charities

There are three main ways for a nonprofit to qualify as a public charity under section 501(c)(3):

- **Automatic.** Certain types of charitable entities are able to automatically qualify as public charities because of the nature of their inherently public activities. These include schools, churches, hospitals, and medical research organizations. These types of entities must meet certain definitional requirements for such entities. These requirements are set forth in Form 1023—the form to apply for IRS recognition of tax-exempt status under section 501(c)(3) and the applicable IRS regulations.[6]
- **Public Support Test.** The most common way to qualify as a public charity is to meet the public support test. Under this test, a nonprofit is able to rely on diverse donation income from a broad base of public support or exempt function income in the form of tuition payments for schools or museum payments, etc.

---

5. I.R.S. Publication 4221 PF, *Compliance Guide for 501(c)(3) Private Foundation,* contains helpful tax compliance information for private foundations.
6. *See* 26 C.F.R. § 1.170A-9.

This is a mathematical test that can be used to establish sufficient public support. There are two, different public support tests for public charities: one is for organizations described in sections 509(a)(1) and 170(b)(1)(A)(vi), and one is for organizations described in section 509(a)(2). These tests measure public support over a five-year period. In general, the 509(a)(1) test requires that the organization receive at least one-third of its support from contributions from the general public (subject to certain limitations on individual contributions), or receive at least 10 percent of its contributions from the general public and demonstrate that it is making significant efforts to increase its public support. The 509(a)(2) test generally requires that the organization receive more than one-third of its support from contributions from the general public and/or from gross receipts from activities related to its tax-exempt purpose (subject to certain limitations on receipts from individual payers). Under this test, an organization can receive no more than one-third of its support from gross investment income and unrelated business taxable income.

- **Supporting Organization.** This is a nonprofit that has been established exclusively to support one or more other public charities. To meet this qualification, it is necessary to meet the requirements of several rules that address the relationship of the nonprofit to other public charities the nonprofit supports. All supporting organizations must pass an organizational test, an operational test, a control test, and a relationship test. Supporting organizations are classified as Type I, Type II, or Type III supporting organizations based on how they satisfy the relationship test.
  - *Organizational Test.* A supporting organization must be organized exclusively for the benefit of, to perform the functions of, or to carry out the purposes of one or more specified section 509(a)(1) or 509(a)(2) organizations. The organization's articles of incorporation must identify the publicly supported organizations on whose behalf the supporting organization is operated. The articles of incorporation of a Type I or Type II supporting organization may des-

ignate and support public charities by class or purpose (as opposed to identifying such organizations by name). In contrast, a Type III supporting organization must identify the supported organization(s) by name. A Type I or Type II (but not a Type III) supporting organization generally may support an organization not organized in the United States. The organization's articles of incorporation may not permit the organization to engage in activities that are not in furtherance of these permitted purposes or to operate to support or benefit any organization other than its specified supported organization(s).

- *Operational Test.* A supporting organization must engage only in activities that support or benefit its supported organization(s). In addition to making direct grants to its supported organization(s), a supporting organization generally is able to make grants or provide services or facilities to: (1) individual members of the charitable class benefitted by its supported organization(s); (2) another supporting organization that supports the same supported organization(s); or (3) a state college or university described in section 511(a)(2)(B) (colleges or universities that are government instrumentalities). Still, any such grants or provision of services or facilities must ultimately support or benefit the supported organization(s), not solely the direct recipients.
- *Control Test.* "Disqualified persons" may not control a supporting organization, whether directly or indirectly. The term "disqualified persons" is defined in section 4946 to include a substantial contributor, a foundation manager, a creator of a trust that is a substantial contributor, a substantial contributor who owns more than 20 percent of the combined voting power of a corporation or other enterprise, a family member of one of the above, and a corporation, partnership, or trust in which one of the above persons owns more than 35 percent of the combined voting power, profits interest, or beneficial interest.
- *Relationship Test.* A supporting organization is classified as a Type I, Type II, or Type III supporting organization based

on the type of relationship it has with its supported organization(s). Type III supporting organizations are further classified as functionally integrated and nonfunctionally integrated.

Supporting organizations, particularly Type III supporting organizations, have been subject to increased regulation since the Pension Protection Act of 2006 due to concerns relating to controlling organizations receiving income from and making loans to supporting organizations.[7]

Limited Liability Companies

The IRS has stated that a limited liability company (LLC) that is a governmental or charitable entity and has two or more tax-exempt members can qualify for tax-exempt status if the LLC satisfies the following conditions:

1. the LLC's organizational documents include a specific statement limiting its activities to one or more exempt (charitable) purposes;
2. the organizational language specifies that the LLC is operated exclusively to further the charitable purposes of its members;
3. the organizational language requires that the LLC's members be charitable organizations, governmental units, or wholly owned instrumentalities of a state or political subdivision of a state;
4. the organizational language prohibits any direct or indirect transfer of any membership in the LLC to a transferee other than a charitable organization, governmental unit, or instrumentality;
5. the organizational language provides that the LLC, interests in the LLC (other than a membership interest), or its assets may only be availed of or transferred to, directly or indirectly, any nonmember (other than a charitable organization, governmental unit, or instrumentality) in exchange for fair market value;
6. the organizational language guarantees that, on dissolution of the LLC, the assets devoted to the LLC's charitable purposes will continue to be devoted to charitable purposes;

---

7. I.R.S. Publication 4221 PC, *Compliance Guide for Public Charities,* contains helpful tax compliance information for public charities.

7. the organizational language requires that any amendments to the LLC's articles of organization and operating agreement be consistent with the general organizational test applicable to charitable organizations;
8. the organizational language prohibits the LLC from merging with, or converting into, a for-profit entity;
9. the organizational language requires that the LLC not distribute any assets to members who cease to be charitable organizations, governmental units, or instrumentalities;
10. the organizational language contains an acceptable contingency plan in the event one or more members ceases at any time to be a charitable organization, a governmental unit, or instrumentality;
11. the organizational language provides that the LLC's exempt members will "expeditiously and vigorously" enforce all of their rights in the LLC and will pursue all legal and equitable remedies to protect their interests in the LLC; and
12. the LLC must represent that all its organizing document provisions are consistent with state LLC laws and are enforceable at law and in equity.[8]

The third condition described above—that the LLC's members be charitable organizations, governmental units, or wholly owned instrumentalities of a state or political subdivision of a state—limits the circumstances under which an LLC can qualify for tax-exempt status.

A single-member LLC whose sole member is a nonprofit corporation with tax-exempt status under section 501(c)(3) generally is not required to seek separate status if it is "disregarded" for tax purposes, resulting in it being treated as a component part of the single member.

In general, contributions to an LLC that is exempt under section 501(c)(3), or is a disregarded entity for federal income tax purposes and is wholly owned by a nonprofit with tax-exempt status under section 501(c)(3), are deductible charitable contributions.[9]

---

8. *See* 2001 EO CPE Text, B. Limited Liability Companies as Exempt Organizations—Update.
9. *See* I.R.S. Notice 2012-52.

APPLICATION FOR TAX-EXEMPT STATUS

As discussed above, the fact that a nonprofit corporation has filed its articles of incorporation with the appropriate secretary of state's office does not automatically mean the entity qualifies for exemption from federal income tax. As discussed below, an application for tax-exempt status might require approval by the IRS.

Determination of Appropriate Tax-Exempt Status

As part of the incorporation process, it is important to evaluate the types of exemptions that would be available for the organization based on its purpose, type of organization, and activities.

Filing of Application for Tax-Exempt Status

For purposes of federal tax exemption, section 508(a) sets forth the requirements for an application for recognition of exemption required by most 501(c) organizations. To obtain tax-exempt status under section 501(c)(3), a public charity must file a Form 1023 with the IRS.[10]

For all other types of tax-exempt entities, the Form 1024 can be filed. Although it is not required that organizations file a Form 1024 to be recognized by the IRS as tax-exempt, an exemption determination letter from the IRS can be helpful in the event the tax-exempt status of the organization is ever challenged in the future, or if a funder requires confirmation of tax-exempt status.

Additional Relevant Forms for Application

To the extent an attorney is to be involved in preparing the application, it is necessary for the attorney to have a preparer tax identification number (PTIN).[11] In addition, a Form 2848, Power of Attorney, should be completed by the organization and submitted with the application. This form authorizes the attorney to represent the applicant before the IRS. These forms are readily accessible on the IRS website.

---

10. As discussed below, some types of church organizations are not required to file applications for tax-exempt status in order to claim such status.
11. *See* I.R.S. Notice 2011-6; 26 C.F.R. § 1.6109-2(d).

Employer Identification Number

As a prerequisite to filing an application for tax-exempt status, it is necessary for the organization to have an employer identification number (EIN). This can be obtained via the IRS website or through a submission to the IRS of a Form SS-4.

Form 1023

The Form 1023 is multiple pages with various schedules and exhibits. The key exhibits are a certified filed copy of the articles of incorporation (that should include provisions describing the tax-exempt purpose of the organization and dissolution provisions to ensure that the assets will be used for charitable purposes) and the bylaws of the organization.

All applicants must complete Parts I through XI of Form 1023. Depending on the type of entity, a schedule may need to be completed as well. Churches must complete Schedule A; schools must complete Schedule B; hospitals must complete Schedule C; and supporting organizations must complete Schedule D.

A guiding principle in terms of responding with substantive answers to questions in the Form 1023 or 1024 is to be transparent and fully describe the organization's current and anticipated future activities. If it recognizes the organization's exemption, the IRS places its stamp of approval in reliance on the activities the applicant described in its Form 1023 or 1024. There may be temptation on the part of the organization to hold back on describing activities if it thinks the IRS will see such activities as an issue. If this is done, the IRS could challenge the conduct or tax exemption in the future as inconsistent with its tax exemption. As a result, it is important the application include a full and complete description of the activities or proposed activities of the organization.

The Form 1023 is a public and permanent record once an exempt status is recognized. As a result, an application should be professional and positive in statements about the organization and its activities. It is also important to keep in mind that the website of the organization is not just the face of the organization to the public at large, but will be reviewed by the IRS when it considers the application for tax-exempt status as well. As a result, the content on the organization's website should be reviewed to ensure the statements on the website are consistent with the statements made in the application. This is also true with respect to any social media sites in which information is provided about the organization.

There are occasional changes to the Form 1023, so there are periodic changes to the Form's instructions. It is important for the attorney to check for any such changes.[12]

When filing the Form 1023, a checklist must be completed. In assembling the Form 1023 or 1024 application, the following are necessary:

- user fee (do not attach to the other documents);
- Form 1023 checklist;
- Form 2848, Power of Attorney (if applicable);
- Form 8821, Tax Information Authorization (if filing, authorize IRS to discuss application with a representative appointed by the power of attorney);
- request for expedited review (if applicable);
- Form 1023 application and Schedules A through H (as applicable; do not include inapplicable blank schedules);
- organizing documents (articles of incorporation, declaration of trust, etc.);
- amendments to the organizing document in chronological order;
- operating document (bylaws, operating agreement, etc.) and amendments;
- documentation of nondiscriminatory policy for schools (if applicable);
- Form 5768 (if desired to elect the section 501(h) expenditure test; not churches); and
- other exhibits (narrative statement, financial data, publications, etc.).

User Fees

There is a user fee for the submission of the application for tax-exempt status. The fee for the Form 1023 is $600. The fee for the Form 1024 depends on the organization's actual or projected annual gross receipts. For organizations that have annual gross receipts that have not exceeded

12. The IRS website (www.irs.gov) sets forth information on the Form 1023, including any changes.

or will not exceed $10,000 for a four-year period, the current fee is $400. For organizations with average annual gross receipts of more than $10,000 over a four-year period, the user fee is $850. Information on the amount of the fee can be obtained on the IRS website. It is recommended that a cashier's check be used for a full Form 1023 rather than a personal check. The IRS will not process the application before the check is cleared.

Timing of Filing of Application

The Form 1023 or 1024 should be filed with the IRS soon after formation.[13] As discussed below, if the application is filed within 27 months from the date of incorporation or formation, the determination of tax-exempt status will be retroactive to the date of incorporation or formation. If the application is filed after 27 months from the date of incorporation or formation, a request may be made in Schedule E to the IRS to have tax-exempt status recognized retroactively to the date of incorporation or formation. If the applicant is making such a request, it is necessary to explain to the IRS why it took the filer so long to file the application. If an exemption is not granted in such circumstances, the tax-exempt status will be effective as of the date of filing the application with the IRS.

It is advisable to submit the application in a manner in which there is some confirmation of receipt, such as certified mail, return receipt requested, or overnight delivery. Such receipt can become valuable if there is ever a question of if and when the IRS received the application.

Expedited Review

The IRS review process can be slow for a Form 1023 or 1024 (after the application has been submitted). Under certain circumstances, the IRS will consider requests for expedited review. These circumstances must be outside the control of the applicant, such as when a third-party grant maker is involved and the nonprofit will lose its funding, and that loss of funding will have a materially negative impact on the nonprofit's operations unless

13. For an organization seeking tax-exempt status under 501(c)(4) of the Internal Revenue Code, the organization must use Form 8976 to provide notice to the IRS within 60 days of its establishment. This form is not a determination that the IRS recognizes the organization as exempt under section 501(c)(4). An application for tax-exempt status is still necessary.

its exempt status is established by a certain date. Requests for expedited review should be made in a separate letter and supported by documentation, such as a letter from the grant maker. If expedited review is requested, an attempt should be made to comply fully with the application requirements and to provide complete information so that it can be approved the first time it is reviewed by an examiner.

Form 1023-EZ

There are two relatively new options available for applying to the IRS for recognition of section 501(c)(3) exemption. As of 2014, it is possible for smaller organizations to file a Form 1023-EZ online with the IRS. This option was created by the IRS due to a backlog in applications for recognition of tax-exempt status. Whereas the Form 1023 is over ten pages of questions plus some schedules, the 1023-EZ is two-and-a-half pages long and requires declarations and representations as opposed to a detailed description of the organization's activities. The main objectives of the 1023-EZ are to minimize the burden on small organizations, reduce the backlog of exemption applications, and shift IRS focus from aspirational activities to actual activities of the organization. The organization must declare that it will have less than $50,000 in revenues each year for the next three years, and that it has less than $250,000 in assets. If an organization meets these requirements, the 1023-EZ is a great option for small nonprofits. The filing fee for the 1023-EZ is $275.

The 1023-EZ option is available only to certain types of public charities; therefore, it is important to review the checklist of permissible entities that may file using the 1023-EZ. Entities not eligible for this option include:

- churches
- schools
- hospitals
- supporting organizations
- international organizations
- private operating foundations
- organizations engaging in joint ventures with for-profit entities

As a first step in completing the 1023-EZ, there is a checklist of 24 yes-or-no questions that must be completed, the answers to which all must be "no" if the organization is to file using the 1023-EZ.

Another important aspect of the Form 1023-EZ is that its questions are designed to determine whether the organization will act in a certain manner to comply with requirements imposed on entities with tax-exempt status under section 501(c)(3). Still, the form does not describe what the actual requirements are for the organization, which presents a counseling challenge for the attorney representing the organization. Unlike the Form 1023, which includes detailed instructions that describe the rules and questions about the activities of the organization, the Form 1023-EZ does not get into such detail; therefore, it is necessary for the attorney for the organization to ensure the organization understands the obligations it is taking on in seeking the tax-exempt status. The attorney also should advise the client seeking tax-exempt status using the Form 1023-EZ that the IRS reviews and examines certain applicants for exemption after they have received an IRS determination of exemption and begun their activities. Moreover, because the determination letter is not based on the IRS's review of a detailed Form 1023 application, there is a question of the reliance value the determination letter will be given by states that rely on IRS determination letters in granting tax-exempt status at the state level and by donors such as private foundations.

The Form 1023-EZ is subject to less scrutiny than the scrutiny to which Form 1023 is subject. As a result, the approval—in the form of an exemption determination letter—is generally more prompt (often within a couple of weeks).

Interactive Form 1023

The IRS also has made available an interactive Form 1023 called the "1023-I" that may be filled out by an entity that is not able to fill out a 1023-EZ, but needs help in completing the full Form 1023. The 1023-I has drop-down menus that assist the preparer in filling out the Form 1023.

Organizations Not Needing to File Applications for Section 501(c)(3) Status

Churches and integrated auxiliaries of churches and conventions or associations of churches and nonprofits with less than $5,000 in annual gross receipts are able to receive tax-deductible contributions even though they never applied for a determination letter from the IRS.

Effective Date of Tax-Exempt Status and Receipt of Tax-Deductible Contributions

Assuming that the entity files for tax-exempt status within 27 months of incorporation, the grant of tax-exempt status generally will be effective retroactively to the date of the incorporation of the nonprofit. During the period of time while the entity is waiting for a determination by the IRS on its tax-exempt status application, it can let donors know that it has applied for tax-exempt status. It is important, however, that donors be told that an application is pending so they understand it is the donors' risk if the tax-exempt status is denied, and the donors have deducted contributions to the organization as charitable contributions.

Public Disclosure and Access

Both Forms 1023 and 1024 and the IRS determination letter are publicly available documents and must be made available for public inspection and disclosure upon request in a manner similar to the requirements imposed on the Form 990, as discussed below. A main difference is that Forms 1023 and 1024 and the determination letter must be made available for public inspection indefinitely.

Recommendations in Preparing Application for Tax-Exempt Status

Some recommendations in preparing the application for tax-exempt status are as follows:

- The organizational form generally will be a corporation (although it can be another type of organization, such as a trust or unincorporated association). It is important to ensure that the articles of incorporation contain a purpose clause that recites only tax-exempt purposes, as well as a dissolution clause that describes how the assets will be distributed for tax-exempt purposes upon dissolution).[14]

---

14. The IRS has determined that, for some states, the charitable assets are sufficiently protected by state law to the extent that a dissolution clause is

- Attach a complete copy of the organizational documents and all amendments thereto. If the applicant is a nonprofit corporation, it is important to include a complete copy of the articles of incorporation that shows it has been filed with and approved by the state of its incorporation. All amendments to the articles of incorporation also should be attached.
- It is extremely important that the narrative description of the activities of the organization be complete. It is not in the best interests of the organization to "hide the ball" about any aspect of its planned activities. Failure to provide enough information about the organization's activities to demonstrate that it will achieve its exempt purpose may result in the IRS denying the exemption application. It is not enough to restate the purpose of the organization. Instead, it is important to provide a description of the specific activities that will achieve that purpose. In this regard, it is important to consider a "who, what, when, where, why, and how" approach. It is also important to explain past, present, and planned activities. If the activities have not yet begun, it is important to develop plans that provide a clear understanding of how the organization will operate.
- The application must list all directors even if they are not compensated. For each of the principal officers and members of the board of directors listed in the Form 1023, it is important to identify the name, mailing address, title and position, and annual compensation (if any). Although address information is required, it is not necessary to provide home addresses. Instead, the organization's address may be used for each director.
- It is acceptable for an organization to compensate officers and directors so long as the compensation is reasonable, but the IRS may want to know enough information on how compensation is determined to be comfortable with the payments to be made to the insiders.
- The process for setting the compensation is important not only for purposes of avoiding prohibited private benefit and inurement, but

---

unnecessary. Even in those states, however, it is best to include the clause to ease the application process.

also for purposes of establishing reasonable compliance with the IRS intermediate sanctions rules (section 4958), as explained below.

- Family and business relationships are a concern for the IRS and must be disclosed.
- The IRS is attentive to an organization that is a successor to another organization. As a result, there are questions on the Form 1023 that address these circumstances.
- Foreign activities can raise red flags for the IRS on a number of grounds and trigger IRS inquiries. Important considerations include ensuring the activity is charitable, determining whether charitable donations are being made to and for the use of a U.S. charity (and not just using the U.S. charity as a pass-through for contributions to a foreign organization), and confirming compliance with the Patriot Act.
- Public charity versus private foundation status is addressed in Part X of the application.
- Advance rulings on public charity status, which were once available, are now obsolete.
- Place the applicant's name and EIN at the top of each page to avoid any confusion as to where the page belongs.
- For attachments, reference the specific Part and line number of the application to which the attachment relates.
- Tapes, recordings, or other electronic media generally are not acceptable attachments unless accompanied by a transcript. Similarly, if any exhibit is not in English, include a translation.
- Include the correct user fee. As noted above, the user fee varies depending upon the type of application that is submitted.
- All required pages must be completed in the application. As noted above, the Form 1023 has various schedules that must be filled out by particular types of nonprofits.
- Include the month the organization's annual accounting period ends. The accounting period ending date on the application should match the accounting period ending date provided in the bylaws of the organization, on financial statements, and on any prior returns filed.
- Include all financial data. The instructions to Form 1023 set forth a description of the information that must be provided as part of the application.

The application must be signed by an officer, director, trustee, or "other officer duly authorized to sign such returns."[15] A principal officer generally is the president, vice-president, secretary, or treasurer. The person signing the application must indicate his or her title or authority to sign. A taxpayer's representative may not sign the application. An original signature is required.

In the event an application for tax-exempt status is denied, there are appeal rights that may be exercised by the applicant.[16]

FORM 990 INFORMATION RETURN REPORTING

A nonprofit corporation claiming tax-exempt status needs to file informational returns with the IRS on an annual basis.

Entities Required to File the Form 990

With some exceptions, a nonprofit corporation with tax-exempt status under section 501(a) is required to file annually a Form 990-series information return. Some tax-exempt entities that are exempt from such filing requirement include:

- churches (unless they incur unrelated business income in a given tax year, in which case they must file Form 990-T for that year)
- integrated auxiliaries of churches
- certain church-affiliated schools and mission societies
- certain governmental and political organizations
- private foundations (which file the Form 990-PF)
- organizations with gross receipts under $200,000 and total assets under $500,000 (which file the Form 990-EZ, or 990-N if gross receipts in the last three years have averaged $50,000 or less)

Types of Form 990-Series Returns

There are a series of Form 990 returns. Section 6033 requires most organizations to file a Form 990. The series includes the following forms:

---

15. *See* 26 C.F.R. § 1.6062-1.
16. *See* I.R.S. Publication 557, *Tax-Exempt Status for Your Organization.*

- Form 990—the main annual information return that must be filed by a mid-size to large tax-exempt entity unless it is exempt from filing a Form 990-series return;
- Form 990-EZ—the short-form version that is for small, nonprofit organizations;
- Form 990-PF—the form for private foundations; and
- Form 990-N—electronic notice that can be filed only by the smallest tax-exempt organizations.[17]

Form 990-N (e-Postcard)

The Form 990-N, which is also called the "e-Postcard," is a creation of the Pension Protection Act of 2006. An organization may file the Form 990-N if its annual gross receipts are normally $50,000 or less, averaged over the past three years. There are certain organizations that cannot file the e-Postcard even if the organization meets the gross receipts requirement. These include organizations that are part of a group return and organizations that voluntarily file the Form 990 or 990-EZ.

There is a special rule for the Form 990-N if an organization is in its first or second year of operation. If it is in the first year of operation, the 990-N filing threshold is $75,000. If it is in its second year of operation, the 990-EZ filing threshold is $60,000 averaged over its first two years.

The Form 990-N is designed to be simple to fill out. It asks only basic information, such as the name, physical address, EIN, website address (if one exists), and the name and address of a principal officer. If the organization has dissolved or is in the process of dissolving, it must check a box that it is terminating. The Form 990-N must be e-filed through the IRS website.[18]

Commencement of Filing of Form 990

Form 990-series return filing requirements commence as soon as an organization holds itself out as tax-exempt. This is true even if the organization

---

17. *See* I.R.S. Publication 4939, *Annual Form 990 Filing Requirements for Tax-Exempt Organizations*.
18. *See* www.irs.gov/eo.

has not yet filed for tax-exempt status with the IRS. As a result, the Form 990 should be filed while the Form 1023 is pending for each year the entity is in existence.

Purpose of Form 990

The Form 990 is the main tool used by the IRS to promote and confirm compliance with applicable tax laws. The Form 990 is not a tax return because tax-exempt organizations do not pay any taxes using Form 990. Still, there are some situations in which taxes may be due from the tax-exempt entity as a result of unrelated business taxable income.[19] In such situations, the organization also must file a Form 990-T, which is a tax return and is filed in addition to—and not in lieu of—the Form 990.

In 2008, the IRS completely redesigned the Form 990 to be a more expansive information return. The Form 990 previously was a form used to report financial information with some yes-or-no questions. Since the redesign, the Form 990 has been expanded to be a return for reporting programs, activities, related organizations, transactions with insiders, and information about how the organization is governed. The redesigned Form 990 also requires information about the financial condition of the organization.[20]

Information Reported on Form 990

The following information is required to be reported on a full Form 990:

- activities and operations (i.e., what does the organization actually do? Is it carrying out its exempt purposes, and is it operated exclusively for exempt purposes? This provides an opportunity for filers to tell their story);
- financial information (i.e., assets, revenue, and expenses);
- compensation (of officers, directors, key employees, highest compensated employees, and independent contractors);

---

19. *See infra* "Unrelated Business Income Tax."
20. The IRS website has helpful information on which annual return must be filed by exempt organizations. *See* www.irs.gov/charities-non-profits/annual-reporting-and-filing.

- relationships and transactions with related organizations and interested persons;
- governance policies and procedures (many questions relate to "best practices"; the IRS believes that a well-governed organization is more likely to be compliant with applicable tax laws); and
- other questions regarding compliance with federal tax-exempt law and IRS filing requirements.

All filers must complete the core Form 990 and at least one or more of the schedules. The majority of filers will complete only a few of the schedules. The most commonly filed schedules are Schedule A, Public Charity Status and Public Support; Schedule B, Contributors; Schedule D, Supplemental Financial Statements; Schedule G, Fundraising or Gaming Activities; Schedule I, Grants or Other Assistance in the United States; and Schedule O, Supplemental Information.

The Form 990-EZ requires less reporting and has fewer schedules. It does not ask information about related organizations. It also asks significantly fewer questions about governance.

Preparation Recommendations

Recommendations for completing a Form 990 include the following:

- Commence the process of information-gathering well in advance of return preparation and filing.
- The preparer cannot operate in a vacuum. It is important to involve program staff, finance, management, and legal.
- Take steps to satisfy the "reasonable efforts" standard. Provide questionnaires to key personnel (including officers, directors, and key employees) to obtain information needed for compensation, independent director, and interested party transaction questions.
- Consider following the Sequencing List (General Instruction C) in completing the form.
- Preliminary considerations should include: (1) 501(c)(3)'s: private foundation (Form 990-PF) or public charity (Form 990); (2) a determination of related organizations; (3) a determination of officers, directors, and key employees; and (4) reference to a glossary for definitions and key terms.

- Do not forget to complete and file Schedule O. This is the only schedule that all 990 filers must file.
- Highlight accomplishments. Tell the organization's story, and show how the organization serves the public and justifies its tax exemption.
- Consider e-filing because it simplifies preparation and reduces errors.
- Use Form 990 as a roadmap and educational tool because it reflects the most applicable areas of tax-exempt law and asks questions relevant to compliance with such areas as: (1) private benefit/inurement; (2) unreasonable compensation; (3) unrelated business income; (4) lobbying/political campaign activity; and (5) policies/governance issues.

In order to avoid filing an incomplete form, it is necessary to:

- answer each question unless instructed otherwise;
- make an entry on every line requiring an amount to be reported (even if zero);
- provide explanations as instructed;
- complete all applicable schedules;
- do not add attachments unless instructed; and
- sign the return (return must be signed by the president, vice-president, treasurer, assistant treasurer, chief accounting officer, or other authorized corporate officer).

Group Return

A consolidated return normally is not permissible. The main exception is where a nonprofit has received a group exemption ruling from the IRS. A group exemption ruling is available for a group of organizations that are affiliated with a central organization. A group exemption letter has the same effect as an individual exemption letter except that it applies to more than one organization.[21] In such circumstances, the group exemption parent may file a Form 990 group return to cover the activities of some or all of the entities covered by the group exemption.

---

21. *See* I.R.S. Publication 4573, *Group Exemptions*.

Filing Deadlines

The filing deadline for a Form 990 is the 15th day of the fifth month following the close of the organization's tax year. This means that a calendar year organization must file by May 15 of the following year. The organization may file Form 8868 with the IRS to request an automatic six-month extension to file the return.

Electronic Filing

The Form 990 must be filed electronically by an organization that has total assets equal to or greater than $10 million, and that files 250 or more IRS returns in a year (including all income, excise, employment tax, and information returns combined).

As a practical matter, however, a significant percentage of organizations e-file their Form 990 returns even though they are not required to do so. Moreover, e-filing will help the organization correctly file the document because the IRS e-file system will screen and reject filings with certain deficiencies.

Penalties for Nonfiling

The failure to file an information return (or complete and accurate return) by the filing deadline may result in penalties of:

- $20 a day, not to exceed the lesser of $10,000 or 5 percent of annual gross receipts for organizations with $1 million or less in annual gross receipts.
- $100 a day, not to exceed $50,000 for organizations with more than $1 million in annual gross receipts.

If more than one return has not been timely, completely, or accurately filed, the penalties apply separately to each of the returns (e.g., Form 990 and Form 990-T).

The failure to file a required electronic notification or 990-series information return for three consecutive years will result in the organization's tax-exempt status automatically terminated pursuant to section 6033(j). In addition, contributions to automatically revoked organizations are not deductible after the date of IRS publication of the revocation. The IRS maintains a website for those organizations that have had their tax-exempt status automatically revoked.[22]

The IRS does not have discretion to reverse an automatic revocation, although it can undo an erroneous auto-revocation notice (e.g., if the organization actually filed a Form 990-series return during the three-year period or was not required to file). In addition, the IRS has the discretion to abate penalties for late filing or nonfiling. If the organization can show good cause as to why the filing was not timely, the IRS can completely abate the penalties. As a result, if a client organization has received a penalty notice, it is worth submitting a request for an abatement showing reasonable cause for late filing.

Public Disclosure and Access

Exempt organizations must make available for public inspection, and disclose upon request, Form 990, 990-EZ, 990-PF, and 990-T for three years after their filing due date.[23] The forms must be made available for public inspection at the organization's principal, regional, and district offices during regular business hours. Copies must be provided upon request either in person, by e-mail, or other means unless the organization makes its Form 990-series returns widely available (e.g., via the Internet).

Most Forms 990 are readily accessible online through the websites of organizations such as Guidestar and Foundation Center. There is, however, a lag time between when Forms 990 are filed and when these organizations post the Forms 990 online because it takes the IRS awhile to process the Form 990 and to provide images of the filed forms to those requesting the forms. In addition, all Form 990-N filings can be accessed on the IRS's website at www.irs.gov/eo.

The Form 990 can be of great interest to media outlets, Congress, state regulatory bodies, watchdog groups, and donors.

Failure to comply with the disclosure requirements can result in penalties assessed by the IRS. The failure to provide copies of annual returns is subject to a penalty of $20 per day, not to exceed $10,000 per return. The failure to allow public inspection of an annual return is subject to a penalty of $20 per day per return (with no maximum penalty). There is no penalty

22. *See* www.irs.gov/autorevocationlist.
23. *See* I.R.C. § 6104(d).

for failure to disclose Form 990-N because it is publicly available on the EO Select Check webpage on IRS.gov.

PRIVATE INUREMENT AND BENEFIT

Overview

A basic tenet of section 501(c)(3) is that charitable organizations are organized to benefit the public and that their earnings are not to inure to the private benefit of an individual. The compensation paid or benefits provided to individuals within the organization can violate the section 501(c)(3) inurement prohibition if the compensation is excessive, particularly if paid to the CEO or other officers and directors of the organization.

It is important to recognize that compensation includes more than just the salary of the individual. It includes retirement benefits, housing, car allowances, insurance premiums, and all other economic benefits.

Executive compensation of officers, directors, key personnel, donors, or related persons can cause concern for many parties involved with nonprofits, including the IRS, state attorney general, members of the nonprofit, donors, and members of the public.

Private Inurement

Section 501(c)(3) provides that no part of an organization's net earnings may inure to the benefit of a private shareholder or individual. The prohibition on private inurement also applies to other types of tax-exempt entities, including:

- 501(c)(4)—social welfare organizations
- 501(c)(6)—business leagues, trade associations
- 501(c)(7)—social and recreational clubs[24]

Inurement to "insiders" is prohibited. Insiders include the organization's board members and officers and its employees who exercise substantial influence over the organization. The penalty for inurement is revocation of federal tax-exempt status.

---

24. Although organizations with tax-exempt status under section 501(c)(7) are subject to the private inurement prohibition, the prohibition does not extend to liquidating distributions.

Private Benefit

In addition to the prohibition on private inurement to insiders, section 501(c)(3) also prohibits 501(c)(3) organizations from generating excessive private benefit to any third party. A "private benefit" is a benefit that primarily furthers a private interest rather than the organization's exempt purposes. A tax-exempt organization may have its tax-exempt status revoked in the event that it generates more than incidental private benefit. Private benefit, if any, must be incidental to achieving the exempt purposes of the organization.

Excess Benefit Transactions/Intermediate Sanctions

Under section 4958, the IRS may impose an excise tax on "disqualified persons" who engage in "excess benefit transactions" with section 501(c)(3) public charities and section 501(c)(4) corporations. The penalties imposed under section 4958 are commonly referred to as "intermediate sanctions" because the penalties fall short of the more draconian option of withdrawing the organization's tax-exempt status. An excess benefit transaction is a transaction, such as the payment of compensation or the transfer of property, in which a "disqualified person" receives more than fair market value from the exempt organization or pays the exempt organization less than fair market value for property or services received from the organization.

The IRS defines the term "disqualified person" as any person who, at any time during the five-year period ending on the date of such transaction, was in a position to exercise substantial influence over the affairs of the organization. The term also includes a member of the family of an individual described in the previous sentence, and any entity in which disqualified persons in the aggregate control 35 percent of the voting interests.

For most section 501(c)(3) and section 501(c)(4) organizations, disqualified persons include directors/trustees, officers, and "substantial contributors" to the organization. Disqualified persons also include top management employees. Whether a person has substantial influence over the affairs of the organization, however, is a facts and circumstances test. As a result, the definition is potentially much broader than the above-listed persons.

Penalties for receipt of excess benefit transactions (commonly referred to as "intermediate sanctions") include:

- return of the value of the excessive benefit to the organization;
- an excise tax of either: (1) 25 percent of the value of the excessive benefit if the benefit is returned to the organization prior to the issuance of a notice of deficiency by the IRS; or (2) 200 percent of the value of the excessive benefit if the benefit is returned after the IRS issues a notice of deficiency.

The intermediate sanctions rules also impose a 10-percent tax on any organization manager who knowingly approves an excess benefit transaction. In addition, liability is joint and several and capped at $20,000 per transaction.

In determining whether there is an excess benefit transaction, the reasonableness of compensation and the fair market value of transactions are determined under existing tax law standards.

There is a rebuttable presumption of reasonableness if the transaction with a disqualified person is:

- approved *in advance* by an independent board or committee thereof, comprised of individuals without a conflict of interest;
- who obtained and relied upon appropriate, *objective data as to comparability*; and
- *documented the basis for their determination* contemporaneously in the minutes of the relevant board or committee meeting.

It is important that the decisions on compensation, benefits, and other payments to "disqualified persons" be made by "disinterested individuals."

"Disinterested individuals" are those persons who do not have a conflict of interest. All of the following persons must recuse themselves from a vote regarding such compensation, benefits, or other payments:

- an individual receiving a direct economic benefit from the transaction;
- a family member of a person benefiting from the transaction;

- employees working under the direction of a person benefiting from the transaction; and
- individuals who have a material financial interest affected by the transaction.

In terms of comparability data, it is important that the data used is, in fact, for other entities comparable to the organization in terms of the organizations' location, size, and activities.

It is acceptable to compare an organization's compensation with the compensation paid by similarly situated for-profit organizations. It is also acceptable and prudent to use third-party compensation and valuation reports.

If the procedures for the rebuttable presumption are met, the burden of proving reasonableness shifts to the IRS. Even without the presumption, benefits provided to disqualified persons are not excess benefit transactions if the organization can demonstrate that they are part of a fair market value exchange of goods or services. Nevertheless, a payment or other benefit that the organization provides to a disqualified person can be justified only as reasonable compensation for services if it is clear that the organization intended and made the payments as compensation for services at the time the payments were made.

UNRELATED BUSINESS TAXABLE INCOME

An exempt organization is not taxed on income from an activity that is substantially related to its exempt purpose. Exempt organizations are, however, subject to tax on net income from "unrelated business taxable income," sometimes referred to as UBTI. Unrelated business taxable income is income generated by a tax-exempt organization from: (1) a trade or business that is (2) regularly carried on and that is (3) not substantially related to the organization's exempt purpose, other than to provide funds to carry out that purpose. If the unrelated business income is "substantial," it will jeopardize the tax exemption of the entity. Unfortunately, the Internal Revenue Code and regulations do not provide a threshold level of allowable unrelated business activity.

The exempt organizations that are subject to UBTI tax, also call Unrelated Business Income Tax or UBIT, include, among others: (1) charitable, religious, scientific, and other organizations described in § 501(c), excluding U.S. instrumentalities; and (2) state colleges and universities.

UBTI is addressed in section 511, *et seq.* and 26 C.F.R. § 1.513-1, *et seq.* IRS Publication 598 provides helpful instruction for determining UBTI issues.

Unrelated Trade or Business

UBTI is the income from a trade or business regularly carried on by an exempt organization that is not substantially related to the performance of the organization's exempt purpose or function.[25] It is important to keep in mind that the "source" and not the "destination" or intended use of the income is relevant in determining whether the income is related or unrelated. The fact that UBTI will be used to support the organization's exempt purposes does not exempt the UBTI from tax.

Under section 513(c) and 26 C.F.R. § 1.513-1, a "trade or business" includes any activity conducted for the production of income from selling goods or performing services. A factor that indicates a profit motive is that the activity engaged in by the organization is similar to activities conducted by nonexempt organizations in order to make a profit. A trade or business does not lose its identity as such because it is carried on within a larger aggregate of similar activities. As a result, a trade or business includes not only a complete business enterprise, but also a component activity of a business.

Under section 513(c) and 26.C.F.R. § 1.513-1, a business activity is "regularly carried on" if: (1) the activity is conducted with a frequency and continuity similar to comparable commercial activities of taxable entities; and (2) the activity is pursued in a manner generally similar to such commercial activities. For example, if comparable commercial activities are normally carried on by a taxable entity on a year-round basis, an exempt organization that carries on a similar activity for a period of a few weeks generally would not be deemed engaged in the regular conduct of a trade or business. In contrast, if comparable commercial activities are normally conducted on a limited or seasonal basis by a taxable entity, the conduct of the similar activity by the exempt organization on a limited or seasonal basis likely will constitute the regular conduct of a trade or business.

---

25. *See* I.R.C. § 512(a)(1).

A trade or business will be found to be unrelated if it is not substantially related to the exercise or performance by the exempt organization of its exempt purpose. A trade or business is considered substantially related if the conduct of the activity has a causal relationship to the achievement of the organization's exempt purpose, and that relationship is a substantial one.

In determining whether an activity contributes in a substantial manner to the accomplishment of an organization's exempt purpose, the size and extent of the activity must be considered in relation to the nature and extent of the exempt function that the activity purports to serve. If the activities are, in part, related to the performance of an organization's exempt function, but the activity is conducted on a larger scale than necessary for the performance of that function, the conduct of the part of the business activity in excess of the exempt needs will be an unrelated business.[26]

Under section 513, an unrelated trade or business does not include:

- **Volunteers**—a trade or business in which substantially all (i.e., 85 percent) of the work is performed for the organization without compensation.
- **Convenience exception**—a trade or business that is carried on by a section 501(c)(3) organization or by a state college or university primarily for the convenience of its members, students, patients, officers, or employees.
- **Sale of donated merchandise**—a trade or business of selling merchandise, substantially all (i.e., 85 percent) of which has been received by the organization as gifts or contributions.
- **Distribution of low-cost articles**—activities relating to the organization's distribution of low-cost articles to donors and potential donors if the distribution is incidental to the solicitation of charitable contributions.
- **Qualified sponsorships**—the solicitation and receipt of qualified sponsorship payments. A qualified sponsorship payment is any payment made to an exempt organization by a person engaged in

26. *See* 26 C.F.R. § 1.513-1(d)(3) and I.R.S. Rev. Rul. 76-94.

a trade or business with respect to which there is no arrangement or expectation that the person will receive any "substantial return benefit" from the organization, other than the use or acknowledgment of the name, logo, or product lines of the person's trade or business in connection with the activity of the exempt organization. Substantial return benefit to a sponsor (which results in UBI from sponsorship income) includes: (1) inducement to buy sponsor's product(s) or take other action; and (2) pricing/product information. Consideration that will constitute a substantial return benefit includes: (1) complementary passes; (2) complimentary facility rentals; (3) discount passes and rentals; (4) sponsor recognition in member publications; and (5) marketing sponsor's goods or services. Substantial return benefit does not include publicizing the: (1) logos and slogans of a sponsor; and (2) address and contact information of a sponsor.

- **Convention or trade-show activities**—activities relating to certain conventions and trade shows.
- **Legal, traditional bingo**—a legal bingo game in a state where bingo games are ordinarily not conducted on a commercial basis.

Exclusions from UBTI Treatment

Once it is determined that an organization is deriving income from an unrelated trade or business, the next step is to determine the amount of UBTI. UBTI means gross income derived from any unrelated trade or business regularly carried on by the exempt organization, less the deductions directly related to carrying on such trade or business and subject to the modifications provided in section 512(b). Various items of income are included in, and related deductions are excluded from, the computation of UBTI. The exclusions are passive income items, including, among other things, dividends, interest, annuities, payments with respect to securities loans, income from notional principal contracts, and other income from an exempt organization's ordinary and routine investments. In addition, royalties and all deductions directly connected with royalty income are generally excluded from UBTI treatment. Subject to certain exceptions, rents and related deductions are excluded from UBTI. Gains or losses from the sale, exchange, or other disposition of property generally are also not considered UBTI. There are, however, important exceptions to these exclusions when the income is debt-financed or is acquired subject to debt-financing. Any organization that has business income or a substantial investment portfolio should work with a competent accountant experienced in filing tax returns for nonprofit organizations.

Certain deductions are permitted in computing UBTI, including the net operating loss deduction and a deduction for charitable contributions.

Tax and Filing Requirements

For exempt organizations organized as corporations and state colleges and universities, the tax on UBTI is computed using the corporate tax rates set forth in section 11. For trusts, the tax is computed using the tax rates for estates and trusts set forth in section 1(e).

An organization subject to the tax on UBTI must file Form 990-T if its gross income from unrelated businesses is $1,000 or more in a given tax year.[27]

Exempt organizations are required to make their tax returns and other tax documents available for public inspection. This requirement applies to Forms 990-T filed by a section 501(c)(3) organization.

PROHIBITION ON CANDIDATE INVOLVEMENT IN POLITICAL CAMPAIGNS

Nonprofits with tax-exempt status under section 501(c)(3) are prohibited from directly or indirectly participating in, or intervening in, any political campaign on behalf of (or in opposition to) any candidate for public office. The IRS may revoke an organization's tax-exempt status or require the organization to pay fines if it engages in such activities. Both the organization itself and the individuals responsible for the illegal political campaign activity may be subject to penalties. Below is an overview of the prohibition, including the 2017 Executive Order relating to religious organizations.

Section 501(c)(3) provides that political activity is "participat[ing] in, or interven[ing] in (including the publishing or distributing of statements) any political campaign on behalf of (or in opposition to) any candidate for

27. *See* 26 C.F.R. §§ 1.511-3(b) and 1.6012-2(e).

public office." Whether activities are considered partisan political activities depends on a "facts and circumstances" inquiry.[28]

Some advocacy and political activities are permissible for a public charity that is tax-exempt under section 501(c)(3). Such a nonprofit may express a point of view about an issue, but may not support or oppose a specific candidate. In addition, voter education activities are permissible for a 501(c)(3) organization so long as they do not make biased references to particular candidates or political parties. Timing is important with regard to the permissibility of voter-education activities. For instance, the publication of a newsletter that contains the voting records of congressional incumbents on selected issues important to an organization likely would constitute participation or intervention in a political campaign if distributed to voters during an election campaign. In contrast, if the newsletter were distributed outside the election season, or covered a broad range of issues, the newsletter may be permissible.

A public charity also may invite a candidate for a political office to speak at an event, provided that opposing candidates for the same office are given equal opportunity to speak. The event as a whole may not advocate for a certain candidate.

In addition, a public charity is permitted to conduct voter registration and get-out-the-vote drives. For such activities, it is important that they be conducted in a neutral, nonpartisan manner. As a result, a public charity should not reference a candidate or political party in its voter registration or get-out-the-vote drive. Also, voter-education or registration activities conducted in a biased manner that favors (or opposes) one or more candidates is prohibited under section 501(c)(3).

Other prohibited political campaign activities for a public charity with 501(c)(3) tax-exempt status include: (1) endorsing a candidate for a public office; (2) urging the public to vote for or against a specific candidate; (3) contributing money to an election campaign; (4) forming or supporting a political action committee (PAC); (5) providing mailing lists to candidates;

---

28. I.R.S. Publication No. 4221-PC, *Compliance Guide for 501(c)(3) Public Charities,* contains helpful information on political activities. I.R.S. Rev. Rul. 2007-41 also provides helpful information on the prohibition against political campaign intervention.

(6) "scoring" or "grading" candidates; (7) providing campaign workers to campaigns for public office; and (8) supporting political parties.

Employees and others involved with a public charity are not permitted to use bulletin boards, letterhead, office space, telephones, servers, and computing capacity (including e-mail addresses) and cash of a charity for campaign activities.

In addition to the restrictions on political and lobbying activities that apply to all section 501(c)(3) organizations, private foundations are subject to excise taxes on expenditures for political and lobbying activities.

In May 2017, an Executive Order was issued stating that it will be the policy of the Executive Branch to "vigorously enforce federal law's robust protections of religious freedom." It directed that, to the extent permitted by law, the Department of Treasury not take any adverse action against any individual, house of worship, or other religious organization on the basis that such individual or organization speaks or has spoken about moral or political issues from a religious perspective, where speech or similar character has, consistent with law, not ordinarily been treated as participation or intervention in a political campaign on behalf of (or in opposition to) a candidate for public office by the Department of Treasury. The term "adverse action" is defined in the Executive Order to mean the imposition of any tax or tax penalty; the delay or denial of tax-exempt status; the disallowance of tax deductions for contributions made to entities exempted from taxation under section 501(c)(3); or any other action that makes unavailable or denies any tax deduction, exemption, credit, or benefit.

Organizations with tax exemption under sections 501(c)(4), 501(c)(5), and 501(c)(6) may engage in political campaigns on behalf of or in opposition to particular candidates so long as such activities are not the primary activities of the organizations. A business-expense deduction for any organization dues, however, is permitted only for that portion of dues or other payments not attributed to such lobbying and campaign activities. Regardless of the tax-exempt status, it is important for all organizations to be aware of federal and state campaign finance laws.

LIMITS ON LEGISLATIVE LOBBYING

Nonprofit organizations with tax-exempt status under section 501(c)(3) may not engage in legislative lobbying except to an insubstantial degree. Below is an overview of the lobbying restrictions imposed on section 501(c)(3) entities.

The Internal Revenue Code establishes two standards for measuring an organization's compliance with these limitations, and the organization itself may elect which standard will apply. One test is known as the subjective "substantial part [of activities] test." This test requires that "no substantial part of a charity's activities . . . be carrying on propaganda or otherwise attempting to influence legislation." The wording is vague, and the exact meaning has proven difficult to define. In an attempt to establish a baseline, some courts have concluded that lobbying expenditures in excess of 5 percent of an organization's total expenditures are substantial, but the circumstances surrounding the individual case are also taken into account. If the IRS determines that an organization has engaged in lobbying beyond an insubstantial amount, the IRS may revoke that organization's federal tax-exempt status.

As an alternative, a public charity (other than a church) may elect to be subject to the objective "expenditure test" when determining whether its lobbying activities are permissible. This second test is found in sections 501(h) and 4911 and establishes limits based on a percentage of an organization's exempt purpose expenditures. Chapter 3 of IRS Publication 557, *Tax-Exempt Status for Your Organization*, more thoroughly describes lobbying expenditure limits under the expenditure test. If an organization has elected to be subject to section 501(h), its lobbying limits will be measured by the "expenditure test." If an organization exceeds the limits established under this test, it must pay an excise tax based on the amount exceeding the limit. Generally, exceeding the lobbying limit under the expenditure test results in the organization having to pay a monetary fine and not in the complete loss of the organization's tax-exempt status. Still, a nonprofit can lose its tax-exempt status under the expenditure test if (based on a four year average) it exceeds the annual lobby limits by a certain amount.

The definitions of lobbying relevant to the objective expenditures test that applies to organizations that have made the 501(h) election are contained in the treasury regulations.[29] Two categories of lobbying are identified: direct lobbying and grassroots lobbying. Direct lobbying refers to any attempt to influence any legislation through communication with any member or employee of a legislative body or with any government official or employee who may participate in the formulation of legislation. This includes any legislator, legislator staff member, or other governmental

29. *See* 26 C.F.R. § 56.4911-2.

official when the primary purpose is to influence legislation. The communication must be about pending legislation to constitute lobbying. For ballot measures, the public is treated as the legislature. Note that the focus is on legislative bodies. This does not include judicial, executive, and administrative bodies. As a result, an organization that encourages an executive or administrative body to take a particular action normally will not be considered to have engaged in lobbying for federal tax purposes. Grassroots lobbying, on the other hand, refers to any attempt to influence legislation through an attempt to affect the opinions of the general public or any segment thereof. Grassroots lobbying, within the terms of the Internal Revenue Code, requires: (1) reference to specific legislation; (2) a specific viewpoint on the legislation; and (3) encouragement of the recipient to take action with respect to the legislation. Under section 4911, the allowed expenditures for grassroots lobbying is 25 percent of the allowed amount for lobbying.

Exceptions to lobbying include nonpartisan analysis, study and research, responding to requests for technical advice, and providing information in self-defense.

A section 501(c)(3) organization can elect to qualify under section 501(h) by submitting IRS Form 5768. The organization must also complete Form 990, Schedule C, Part II-A, annually. Organizations that do not elect under section 501(h) will measure lobbying under the "substantial part [of activities] test." Not all 501(c)(3) nonprofit organizations may elect to qualify under section 501(h). The section 501(h) election is not available to churches, an integrated auxiliary of a church, a convention or association of churches, or a member of a group of affiliated organizations that includes a church. Private foundations also cannot make this election. A private foundation is subject to excise taxes on expenditures for lobbying activities.

Section 501(c)(4), 501(c)(5), and 501(c)(6) organizations may engage in an unlimited amount of lobbying so long as the lobbying substantially furthers the exempt purposes of the organizations. In addition, the lobbying and political activity portion of member dues to a section 501(c)(6) organization is not tax deductible by the members of the organization as an ordinary and necessary business expense. The organization has two options in this regard: (1) notify members annually of the amount of dues that are not deductible as a result of the lobbying and political activity expenditures; or (2) pay a proxy tax on those amounts to the IRS.

For nonprofits engaging in lobbying, other federal and state laws must be considered. At the federal level, the Lobbying Disclosure Act, 2 U.S.C. § 1601 *et seq.*, applies to nonprofits if the organization has: (1) at least one employee who is a "lobbyist"; and (2) expenditures of $20,000 or more per six-month period on lobbying activities. A "lobbyist employee" is an employee who makes at least two lobbying contacts and spends at least 20 percent of his or her time on lobbying activities. This act applies only to lobbying on the federal level. Federal lobbying is reported on form LD-2. At the state level, there often are rules regulating lobbying activity that also impose registrations requirements. For large nonprofits with tax-exempt status under section 501(c)(3), there typically is at least one person who meets the registration requirements.

Governance

4

OVERVIEW

The discussion on bylaws in Chapter 3 covered possible provisions relating to the members, directors, and officers. These provisions are important for purposes of the governance of the organization. Governance of nonprofit corporations is controlled by state law. In addition, the IRS and a number of good-governance advisory groups have taken (nonenforceable) positions on what nonprofit board of directors should do and how effective boards should be structured. The IRS has done this in various ways, including requiring tax-exempt organizations to disclose in the Form 990 the answers to numerous questions about certain governance aspects of the organization.

Below is a general description of the roles of the various individuals involved with the governance of nonprofit corporations.

Members

If a nonprofit corporation has members, they function similarly to shareholders of a for-profit corporation by voting on the election of directors and on fundamental transactions involving the nonprofit, such as mergers, sale of assets, and dissolution. Unlike shareholders, however, the members have no ownership interest in the corporation.

As noted above, it is possible that a nonprofit corporation could refer to a group of individuals or entities as "members" for fundraising purposes even when they have no voting rights. It is important to avoid any implication that such "members" have voting rights to appoint board members or approve other matters.

Board of Directors

The directors are responsible for managing the affairs of the organization. In essence, they "direct" the corporation. They are responsible for setting policy and the direction of the corporation. The directors act collectively and not individually. As directors, they do not direct the day-to-day activities of the organization, but rather delegate such duties to senior officers or an executive director and paid staff.

As noted in the discussion on bylaw provisions, the board of directors can act through a meeting (in person or by telephone or other electronic means by which the directors can hear each other) or by written consent. From a governance standpoint, meetings are the preferable method of board action because they allow the board members to discuss issues and benefit from the collective wisdom of the group before making a decision. A written consent, although effective, often occurs without discussion among the board members.

Officers

The officers—typically including a president, secretary, and treasurer—have the responsibility for implementing directives of the board of directors. Whether they are directors who also serve as officers or are staff officers, the officers are responsible for the day-to-day operation of the corporation. The officers (even those who may also be directors) are accountable to the board of directors and report back to the directors on the activities of the organization. The board is responsible for overseeing and directing the officers. Unlike the board of directors, the officers can act individually. As discussed above, it is possible for directors to also be officers, but it is important for them to remember which "hat" they are wearing.

Overriding Authority

It is possible in a nonprofit corporation to have an "overriding authority" that is above the members, board of directors, and officers. This typically arises in the context of religious corporations, with a religious-affiliated person or body assuming a membership role or otherwise holding certain approval powers for specified matters. This also can arise in the context of legacy corporations with a board of visitors' overseers. When such authority exists, it is important to determine whether this person, group, or entity is acting as a member (including approving significant matters approved by the board) or assuming the authority and responsibilities (including fiduciary duties) otherwise assigned to the board of directors. This must be documented in the articles of incorporation or the bylaws of the organization.

Resolving Disputes

Consideration should be given to including in the bylaws or other document a process for resolving disputes among directors, officers, members, and other interested parties. This can help avoid litigation.

Committees

Depending on state law, committees of the board that are to exercise any of the board's authority may need to be composed of only board members or a certain percentage of board members (e.g., a majority of board members). The power of a board to delegate certain powers to a board committee is subject to some restrictions that are typically set forth in the applicable nonprofit corporation act. For example, typical actions that cannot be delegated to committees include approval of dissolutions, mergers, or the sale of all or substantially all of the assets, electing or appointing board members, or adopting or amending the articles of incorporation or bylaws.

An executive committee can be helpful if there is a large board of directors. Such committee typically is empowered to act on behalf of the board between meetings of the board and can have additional responsibilities, including conducting the evaluation and determining or recommending the compensation of the senior executive officer of the organization.

Other typical nonprofit corporation committees include the audit and/or finance committees. Some states require that audit committees exist for nonprofits of a certain size. Finance committees can be given board authority to take action on behalf of the board with regard to financial matters.

Advisory committees are more flexible in that they can be made up of nondirectors and directors. They do not have board authority, but instead implement the decisions of the board or report back to the board, which then makes the final decisions.

Duplicate Boards

Some nonprofits are structured to have more than one governing board. This can cause confusion in terms of each board's responsibility and the fiduciary duties imposed on the directors. To the extent that authority will be delegated to more than one governing board, it is important to identify precisely the responsibilities of each of the governing boards. In addition, to the extent that a nonprofit has assigned responsibility for governance to more than one board, the nonprofit should make it clear which body has ultimate control.

FIDUCIARY DUTIES

Most state nonprofit corporation acts and case law impose certain fiduciary duties on directors of nonprofit corporations. As indicated above, directors are responsible for managing the affairs of the corporation. As such, legal obligations are imposed on the directors in the form of the duty of care and a duty of loyalty. In addition, courts have sometimes recognized a third duty: the duty of obedience (which is frequently considered to be part of the duty of loyalty).

These fiduciary duties apply to all directors, even if they are appointed by or are representative of another group, such as a regional affiliate. In these situations, the directors may bring a different perspective, but they maintain a fiduciary obligation to the nonprofit corporation. As a result, it is important that directors in this situation recognize that they may have overlapping duties (to the organization that appointed them or for which they are serving as a representative, and to the nonprofit) and that potential conflict or dualities of interest situations that might arise as a result.

The following is a brief summary of the fiduciary duties of nonprofit corporation directors.

Duty of Care of Directors

General Standards

Under the duty of care, directors, when becoming informed in connection with their decision-making and oversight functions, are to discharge their duties with the care that a person in a like position would reasonably believe appropriate under similar circumstances.

The duty of care includes two main functions: decision-making and oversight. In terms of decision-making, which usually is in the form of voting on a matter, each director must have sufficient information to be able to make an "informed" vote.

The oversight function relates to the board's responsibility for monitoring the operations of the organization. This means, among other things, that a director should have a general knowledge of the nonprofit corporation's operations, be aware of what the financial records disclose, and take appropriate actions to ensure there are proper internal controls, including compliance programs. A director also should make reasonable inquiry in appropriate circumstances, such as when there is troubling or unclear activity. For example, upon becoming aware of warnings or reports of officer or employee theft or mismanagement, the board should ensure that a proper investigation is made and action taken.

To the extent a director becomes aware of information that is material to the board's discharge of its decision-making and/or oversight functions that the director knows is not already known to other directors, it is incumbent upon the director to disclose the information to the other directors unless doing so would violate a duty imposed under law, a legally enforceable obligation of confidentiality, or a professional ethics rule.[1]

There can be special hazards for attorneys and other experts serving on the board. Such board members could be subject to a higher standard of care by comparison to others with similar expertise. To avoid liability risk, it is advisable for attorneys and other experts on the board to clarify when they are expressing an expert opinion versus a general perspective.

1. *See* Model Nonprofit Corporation Act, Third Edition, § 8.30.

Steps to Take in Meeting Duty of Care

The duty of care involves active participation in the organization. This means that a director should regularly attend meetings of the board and board committees, enter into discussions at such meetings when appropriate, evaluate reports, read minutes (which should be taken at every board and committee meeting), learn about the organization's programs, and review the performance of the senior executive officer and the organization's budget.

An "insider's" tip in terms of meeting the duty of care is to be respectful in asking questions of others.

The "Three Little Bears Rule" applies to the level of information needed to exercise a directors' duty of care. The director should expect and request information in the "just right" form—not too much and not too little—such that it is digestible by the board and the director to understand the issues and make informed decisions. To achieve this goal, the use of dashboards and executive summaries with detailed appendices can be helpful.

A director who is present at a meeting when action is approved by the board is presumed to have agreed to the action unless the director objects to the action.

Under the duty of care, it is not expected that the directors will be involved in the day-to-day activities of the organization. Still, the board of directors should assure that there is a proper delegation of authority to management with clear limits and reporting expectations. The board should receive adequate, regular reports on key operational activities and results. The board should provide feedback—both positive and negative—to management, including expectations for improvement as warranted.

Reliance on Others

In carrying out the duty of care, a director may rely upon others—including committees of the board of directors, attorneys, accountants, and other experts—if the reliance is in good faith. As a result, a director can rely on others for information, and it is not expected that the director must independently verify such information.

There is an exception to the reliance rule in the situation where the director knows or should know that such reliance is unwarranted. To the extent the director has a special expertise in a matter, the director is expected to use such expertise in determining the reasonableness of the reliance. Unquestioned reliance on an expert, which might arise in a situation in which the director fails to review or question reports of management, is not permissible.

The key to reliance is that it is reasonable and that the director reviews the information provided and asks questions when necessary.

Some steps to ensure this is accomplished include: assuring the minutes reflect board engagement, approaching information with a "trust but verify" attitude, reading all of the materials provided, and asking questions or seeking additional information if the director does not understand or identifies anything that may be of concern.

A failure to meet the duty of care standard can result in harm to the organization to reach its potential (and in some cases even to remain viable). It also can result in potential liability if it results in harm to the organization or third parties.

Uniform Prudent Management of Institutional Funds Act

Many states have adopted the Uniform Prudent Management of Institutional Funds Act (UPMIFA), which applies to institutions that are organized and operated exclusively for charitable purposes. UPMIFA provides that, in addition to complying with the duty of loyalty imposed by law other than UPMIFA, each person responsible for managing and investing an institutional fund must manage and invest the fund in good faith and with the care an ordinarily prudent person in a like position would exercise under similar circumstances. In managing and investing an institutional fund, the following factors, if relevant, are to be considered: (1) general economic conditions; (2) the possible effect of inflation or deflation; (3) the expected tax consequences, if any, of investment decisions or strategies; (4) the role that each investment or course of action plays within the overall investment portfolio of the fund; (5) the expected total return from income and the appreciation of investments; (6) other resources of the institution; (7) the needs of the institution and the funds to make distributions and to preserve capital; and (8) an asset's special relationship or special value, if any, to the charitable purposes of the institution.

In addition, UPMIFA provides that management and investment decisions about an individual asset are to be made not in isolation, but rather in the context of the institutional fund's portfolio of investments as a whole and as a part of an overall investment strategy having risk and return objectives reasonably suited to the fund and to the institution. Subject to any specific limitations set forth in the gift instrument or in law, UPMIFA also permits an institution to delegate the management and investment of an institutional fund to an external agent to the extent an institution can prudently delegate under the circumstances.

UPMIFA also provides that, subject to the intent of the donor expressed in the gift instrument, an institution may appropriate for expenditure or accumulate so much of an endowment fund as the institution determines is prudent for the uses, benefits, purposes, and duration for which the endowment fund is established. Similar to the investment standard, in making a determination to appropriate or accumulate, the institution shall act in good faith, with the care that an ordinary prudent person in a like position would exercise under similar circumstances, and, if appropriate, consider the following factors: (1) duration and preservation of the endowment fund; (2) purposes of the institution and the endowment fund; (3) general economic conditions; (4) the possible effect of inflation or deflation; (5) the expected total return from income and appreciation of investments; (6) other resources of the institution; and (7) the investment policy of the institution.

Duty of Loyalty of Directors

General Standard

State nonprofit corporation law also requires that each member of the board of directors of the corporation, when discharging the duties of a director, acts in good faith and in a manner that the director reasonably believes to be in the best interests of the corporation. This means a director is required to exercise his or her power in the interest of the nonprofit corporation, and not in his or her own interest or the interest of another person or entity. As a result, a director should avoid using his or her position in a manner that would result in pecuniary gain for the director or a member of the director's family. The duty of loyalty can be viewed as covering both conflict of interest and corporate-opportunity situations.

Conflict of Interest

Conflict of interest transactions involving directors are not necessarily prohibited for a nonprofit corporation. In fact, they can be beneficial if a director is able to offer a good or service to a nonprofit corporation at no charge or at a price that is below fair market value. Still, conflict of interest situations can be detrimental to a nonprofit corporation when they cause the nonprofit to pay for a good or service in an amount that exceeds a fair price or advantages the director to the detriment of the organization. As a result, it is important that conflict of interest situations be managed through a process that helps prevent directors from taking advantage of the entity as a result of their position on the board.

Nonprofit corporation acts generally provide a "safe harbor" for handling these situations: A conflict of interest transaction is not voidable by the corporation on the basis of the director's interest in the transaction if the transaction was fair at the time it was entered into or is approved as follows:

- the material facts of the transaction and the director's interest are disclosed or known to the board of directors or a committee of the board of directors, and the board of directors or committee (excluding any interested directors) authorized, approved, or ratified the transaction; or
- if the organization has voting members, the material facts of the transaction and the director's interest were disclosed or known to the members that (excluding any interested members) authorized, approved, or ratified the transaction.

As noted above, under certain circumstances, a transaction between a nonprofit corporation and its director (or an entity in which the director has a financial interest) may be acceptable and beneficial to the corporation. In order to allow (and protect from challenge) such types of transactions, the process set forth above should be followed. This can be accomplished through a conflict of interest policy or bylaws provision that incorporates the requirements set forth above. A policy also might require that the interested board member be excluded from participation in the approval process. For any transaction involving a conflict of interest, it is important that the process followed by the corporation in handling the matter be documented in the minutes of the meeting.

When considering possible transactions in which there is a conflict of interest, it is also important to consider the public perception of the transaction (even if the director and nonprofit has complied with the applicable conflict of interest or business-opportunity requirements). Good questions to ask are: "What would this look like if it were on the front page of the local newspaper?" Is this something that the nonprofit corporation and director(s) will be proud of if it becomes public? It is best to ask how the transaction will benefit the organization.

Director compensation falls under the category of conflict of interest because it is the directors who are approving the compensation (unless another group or body, such as members, approve the compensation). As directors consider the compensation amount, it is important to keep in mind that such compensation is public record if the nonprofit is tax-exempt and files a Form 990.

Corporate Opportunity

The second type of situation that might involve the duty of loyalty is when a director becomes aware of an opportunity made available to the corporation that the director would like to pursue for his or her own personal benefit or the benefit of others unrelated to the entity. A director who engages in a transaction that the director should reasonably know may be of interest to the corporation should disclose the transaction to the board of directors in sufficient detail and in adequate time to enable the board to act or decline to act with regard to such transaction. Some states have "corporate opportunity" or "business opportunity" provisions in their nonprofit acts that require a two-step process of full disclosure to the board of directors of the potential opportunity and the interested director's nonparticipation in voting on the opportunity.

Confidentiality

In addition, the duty of loyalty requires that, in the regular course of business, a director not disclose information about the corporation's legitimate activities unless they are already known by the public or are of public record. This duty of confidentiality exists because the disclosure of the information could be detrimental to the interests of the organization.

Obedience to the Nonprofit Purposes and Mission

Under the duty of loyalty, nonprofit directors have been determined to owe a duty to the purpose (and/or mission) set forth in the entity's organizational documents, such as the articles of incorporation. In addition, directors must comply with state and federal laws that relate to the organization and the manner in which it conducts its business. One reason for imposing the duty of obedience on directors is that donors rely on an organization's faithfulness to its purpose when making donations. [2]

Role of Management in Supporting the Directors' Fulfillment of Duties

The management of the organization plays a significant role in ensuring that the directors fulfill their fiduciary duties. To the extent the management includes officers of the organization, they also have fiduciary duties to the organization.

It is important to keep in mind that the success of the organization is a "team effort," and that an effective interrelationship between management and the board in assuring good governance is essential.

For management, it is important that the directors be provided relevant and digestible information. For the board, it is important to allow management to manage the day-to-day operations with the board providing oversight and feedback. It is incumbent upon the board to ensure that there is an effective review process for the senior executive and other key officers/employees.

LIABILITY OF DIRECTORS, INDEMNIFICATION, AND D&O COVERAGE

Liability Shields

Many state nonprofit corporation acts include provisions protecting directors and officers from liability. Under the Model Nonprofit Corporation Act,

---

2. Directors also must obey the organization's rules and directives. For example, if the board adopts a policy that only certain authorized directors may speak directly to the media about the nonprofit's mission-related activity, violation of this policy could be treated as a breach of the duty of obedience.

Third Edition (MNCA), a director or officer of a charitable nonprofit corporation is not personally liable in that capacity for any action taken or failure to take any action except liability for any of the following: (1) the amount of any financial benefit to which the person is not entitled; (2) an intentional infliction of harm on the corporation or member; (3) a violation of the unlawful distribution provision; and (4) an intentional violation of criminal law. The MNCA allows for the same protection for other types of nonprofit corporations (such as mutual benefit corporations) that include a provision in their articles of incorporation. In some states, directors are entitled to immunity protection only if they receive no or minimal compensation.

Many state nonprofit corporation acts also include the "business judgment" rule that helps protect a director against a claim so long as the director's conduct has been shown to be in good faith and in a manner reasonably believed to be in the nonprofit's best interest, and with independent and informed judgment. It is applicable in other states through case law development.

Directors also have possible protection under the Federal Volunteer Protection Act of 1997. The act provides civil liability protection for unpaid or minimally paid (no more than $500 annually) nonprofit volunteers if: (1) the volunteer was acting within the scope of his or her responsibilities; (2) the volunteer was properly licensed, certified, or authorized to engage in the activity or practice (if required by the state in which the damage occurred), and those activities were within the scope of the volunteer's responsibilities; (3) the harm was not caused by willful or criminal misconduct, gross negligence, reckless misconduct, or a conscious, flagrant indifference to the rights or safety of the individual harmed by the volunteer; and (4) the harm was not caused by the operation of a motor vehicle, aircraft, or other vehicle for which an operator's license or insurance is required by the state.[3]

Although the immunity statutes can be helpful in protecting the ultimate liability of a director or officer of a nonprofit corporation, they do have limitations. In particular, they do not protect these individuals from being sued and incurring attorney's fees and other out-of-pocket expenses incurred in their representation.

3. *See* 42 U.S.C. §§ 14501–14505.

Indemnification

It is common for state nonprofit corporation acts to allow nonprofit corporations to indemnify their officers and directors. Older nonprofit acts also expressly provide for the indemnification of employees, whereas new versions do not address this point because indemnification of employees, while permissible, is not a topic to be addressed in a nonprofit corporation act. The general standard for indemnification often is that the individual acted in good faith and in a manner in which the individual reasonably believed either that the individual's conduct was in the best interest of the organization, or that it was not at least opposed to the best interests of the organization.

Mandatory indemnification by a nonprofit corporation typically is provided for in the bylaws when the director has been wholly successful, on the merits or otherwise, in the defense of any proceeding in which the director was a party because the director is or was a director of the nonprofit.

In addition, the nonprofit corporation acts generally allow a nonprofit corporation to indemnify and advance costs and reimburse its directors and officers for costs involved in defending a legal action in the person's capacity as a director or officer.

The MNCA allows a nonprofit corporation to mandate indemnification to the same extent as the liability shield provides protection if so specified in the articles of incorporation. As a result, a nonprofit corporation can (but is not required to) indemnify its directors for any actions or inactions except in the four limited circumstances discussed above where the liability shield is not applicable.

It is important to recognize that the practical availability of indemnification protection for the officers and directors of a nonprofit corporation depends on the resources of the organization. As a result, although the provision may be helpful to the corporation and its directors, it may be of little value in the end if the organization does not have the funds to reimburse directors, and no insurance coverage is available.

Directors and Officers Liability Coverage

Many nonprofits purchase directors and officers (D&O) insurance. In general, D&O insurance provides coverage for the actions and inactions of the organization's directors and officers, including intentional actions of these individuals. Most claims under D&O coverage relate to employment matters, including wrongful termination claims. In addition, D&O insurance is important for purposes of protecting against governance-type liability (relating to claims arising from board or officer decisions) and fiduciary liability, which can arise in a variety of situations, including conflict of interest situations where there is an improper personal financial benefit.

An important consideration with regard to D&O insurance is the amount of the deductible. There may be a lower deductible for directors and officers than for the organization. In addition, given the frequency of employment-related claims, it is important to ensure that the D&O policy covers such types of claims.

By having such coverage, the directors, officers, and the organization are not solely reliant on the resources of the organization to indemnify the directors for any costs incurred as a result of legal actions. Although the liability shield provides protection to directors, officers, members, and other volunteers, it does not prevent these individuals (or the corporation) from being sued and incurring attorney's fees and other legal costs, which can be covered by D&O coverage. D&O coverage also can provide protections to directors and officers without the need of relying on the assets of the organization, which would be the case if the nonprofit was indemnifying the individual.

FORM 990 GOVERNANCE ISSUES

Starting in 2009, the full Form 990, which must be completed by tax-exempt nonprofits that have at least $200,000 in annual gross receipts or $500,000 in total assets at the end of the tax year, began asking questions about the governance of the nonprofit corporation, including specific types of governance policies.[4]

The Form 990 typically is changed each year by the IRS at least incrementally. As a result, it is important that the practitioner be aware of the updated form. In addition, the instructions issued by the IRS for the Form

4. Certain kinds of religious, governmental, and political tax-exempt organizations are exempt from filing the full Form 990, 990-EZ, or 990-N (e-post card). In addition, if not exempt, smaller entities are required to file the Form 990-N or 990-EZ, which do not ask governance questions. Private foundations file the Form 990-PF, which also does not ask governance questions.

990 are helpful in understanding the type of information the IRS is seeking. They also provide insight on the IRS's views of good governance structures and practices and areas of concern.

Part VI of the Form 990 is the core section on governance disclosures; however, Part VII addresses compensation disclosures, and Part XII addresses financial statements and reporting—all of which relate to governance matters. An important point to remember is that the Form 990 is no longer something for only accountants to prepare. Review by an attorney or other person familiar with the organization's governance structure often is needed to assure that all governance-related questions are answered correctly.

There is a question as to why the IRS focuses on governance issues, given that it is not a governmental authority responsible for the governance of the organization. The IRS response is that it believes good governance principles are tied to tax compliance. The problem is that there is no evidence that what the IRS considers to be good governance actually results in better run organizations.

It is important to understand that the IRS is not prescribing a right or wrong answer in Part VI of the Form 990. It is an information return. Still, the form is a public document that will be viewed by members of the public, including members of the press, grant-making organizations, and government agencies, including the IRS and states. Moreover, the IRS wants to be able to determine whether good governance principles are, in fact, implemented by an organization.

Although the form does not prescribe a right or wrong answer, it is clearly structured to motivate an entity to answer "yes" to many of the questions relating to policies and procedures the organization has in place.

Some of the other questions asked in the Form 990 relate to the following:

- number of "voting members" of the "governing body" at the end of the tax year;
- number of "independent" voting members of the governing body;
- "family relationships or business relationships" among officers, directors, trustees, or "key employees";
- any delegation of control over management duties customarily performed by/under the supervision of officers, directors, trustees, key employees to a management company, or others;

- "significant changes" to governing documents since the last Form 990 was filed;
- whether the organization became aware during the year of a "significant diversion of assets";
- whether the organization has "members or stockholders";
- whether the organization has members, stockholders, or others who may elect members of the governing body;
- whether any of the governing body's decisions are subject to approval by members, stockholders, or others;
- whether the organization has local chapters, branches, or affiliates and, if so, whether it has written policies or integrated purposes clauses to ensure their operations are consistent with the organization;
- whether the Form 990 has been provided to all members of the governing body before filing (it is necessary to describe the process for such review);
- whether the organization has a conflict of interest policy and, if so, whether (1) officers, directors, or trustees and key employees are required to disclose annually their potential conflicts; and (2) the organization regularly and consistently monitors and enforces compliance (if so, it is necessary to describe the process used);
- whether the organization has a written whistleblower policy;
- whether the organization has a written document retention and destruction policy;
- whether the process for determining the compensation for the CEO, executive director, or top management official and other officers and key employees includes a review and approval by independent persons, comparability data, and contemporaneous substantiation of the deliberation (if so, the process must be described);
- whether the organization invested in/contributed assets to/participated in a joint venture or similar arrangement with a taxable entity during the year and, if so, whether the organization adopted a written policy or procedure requiring evaluation of participation in the joint ventures under applicable federal law and took steps to safeguard exempt status with respect to joint-venture arrangements;
- list the states in which a copy of the Form 990 is required to be filed;

- whether the Form 990 (and specified other IRS filings) is made available for public inspection via the organization's website, another website, or upon request;
- whether (and, if so, how) the organization makes its governing documents, conflict of interest policy, and financial statements available to the public (note, however, that under state and federal law, a nonprofit generally is not required to make the bylaws, conflict of interest policy, or financial statements available to the public—only the Form 990 and the Form 1023 or 1024 are required to be disclosed—whereas the articles of incorporation is a public document available from the appropriate secretary of state office); and
- name, physical address, and telephone number of the person who possesses the organization's books and records.

BOARD POLICIES

Effective board governance dictates that a nonprofit corporation have policies and follow them. There is not a "one size fits all" set of policies that a nonprofit corporation is to adopt and implement. As a result, there is significant risk for organizations that take a set of policies off the Internet and adopt them without considering their impact on the organization. Instead, it is important that the nonprofit consider its activities, including any services it offers, and the risks associated with its activities to develop a set of customized policies that help minimize the risks from occurring. If prepared properly, the policies can provide a good road map for compliance with various legal requirements. It is extremely important that the policies make sense to the organization and that the organization be able to comply with them. The only thing worse than having no policies is having a set of policies that are not followed. Below is a description of common policies for a nonprofit corporation.

Mission Statements

Many nonprofit organizations have mission statements that are developed from a strategic planning process. The IRS has expressed a belief that organizations should have a mission statement. The mission statement should be simple and easily understood, with the statement setting forth the goals and aspirations of the organization. A mission statement can be easily modifiable based on the operations of the organization.

The mission statement is not the same thing as the "purpose" of the organization, which is set forth in the governing documents (articles of incorporation and/or bylaws) of the organization. The "purpose" limits what the organization can do. The mission statement must be consistent with the purpose provision in the articles of incorporation, but address what the organization is currently doing.

The mission statement typically is approved by the board of directors. It is not usually included in the organization's articles or bylaws, but may be on its website. The purpose provision, because it is part of the articles of incorporation, must be approved by the board and possibly the members of the nonprofit corporation. In addition, any amendment to the purpose provision requires a filing with the secretary of state's office because it constitutes an amendment to the articles of incorporation.

Compensation

A compensation policy is important for purposes of ensuring compliance with compensation restrictions imposed under the Internal Revenue Code. In addition, as discussed above, the Form 990 asks questions regarding the existence of a process for determining compensation of the directors, officers, and key employees, and the actual compensation of these individuals must be disclosed in the Form 990.

The intermediate sanctions law, which was adopted in 1996, gives the IRS authority to impose significant penalties on organizations, their governing boards, and employees in situations in which compensation is determined to be unreasonable.[5] The concern of the law is to avoid situations where someone has control or the ability to exert influence over the organization to the detriment of the organization. In order to comply with intermediate sanctions law requirements on compensation, the following steps should be described in a compensation policy and closely followed by the organization when determining compensation of directors (if any), officers, and key employees:

5. *See supra* Chapter 3, "Private Inurement and Benefit," Excess Benefit Transactions/Intermediate Sanctions.

- review and approval by independent persons, such as independent members of the board of directors (who do not have a financial interest in the determination);
- use of comparability data supporting a determination that the compensation determined by the board is reasonable (this can include independent salary survey information); and
- contemporaneous substantiation in the form of written minutes or a memo or report.[6]

Reimbursement Policy for Business and Travel Entertainment

This policy should apply to officers, directors, and key employees and may apply to all employees. It is important to ensure that, if the nonprofit is reimbursing any director, officer, or employee expenses, the terms of the reimbursement are made clear. It also is important that receipts are attached to each reimbursement request and appropriate review processes are in place to ensure that the expenses are legitimate. A third party should approve any reimbursement.

If a nonprofit is to have credit cards that it pays directly, special care must be taken to assure that only legitimate charges are paid by the organization.

Conflict of Interest

This is a policy that every nonprofit should have. This type of policy must be tailored based on the activities of the organization to identify what kinds of activities by officers, directors, or key employees, in addition to what typical issues (such as providing goods or services to the organization), might trigger a conflict of interest issue. For example, for an art museum, a conflict of interest policy might address the acquisition of art. For a school, the policy might address tuition reimbursement or reduction.

6. *See* I.R.C. § 4958. It is necessary to set forth the determination and include in the minutes a description of the approval process and reasons for determining the reasonableness of the payments. In addition, the approval of the compensation for the chief executive officer, chief operating officer, chief financial officer, other executive officers, and directors should follow this process. In some states, the CEO's and CFO's compensation is required to be approved by the board of directors. *See* California Nonprofit Integrity Act, Cal. Gov. Code §§ 12585–12586.

A key component of a conflict of interest policy is requiring disclosure by the interested parties. A form signed on an annual basis by directors, officers, and key employees disclosing any potential conflicts can be helpful to the organization in identifying conflict situations.

The IRS has prepared a sample conflict of interest policy that is part of the instructions to Form 1023. Although the form is helpful in describing a process for handling conflicts, it does have some drawbacks. First, even if an organization complies with the form of the policy, it still may not be in compliance with section 4958 (excess benefit transactions). Second, the sample policy does not account for any particular requirements imposed under state law for conflict of interest transactions. Finally, the IRS example policy does not reference "key employees." The Form 990, however, asks if the organization has adopted a conflict of interest policy that covers directors, officers, and key employees.

Board Member Independence

This policy is important for handling conflict of interest situations as well as responding to the questions on board member independence in the Form 990. The IRS defines such independence to mean a director that does not receive any salary or other financial benefit from the organization (other than compensation for services as a director). Such criteria may be difficult to determine and implement. Moreover, it is important to recognize that a director may be "interested" (and therefore not "independent") in one area, but not all areas.

It is possible that a director can arrange to have a good or service made available to the nonprofit at a price favorable to the nonprofit. Where the director has an ownership interest in the business offering such good or service, the director lacks independence with respect to such transactions. Although the transaction may be beneficial for the organization, the director and the organization must be ready to justify the transaction.[7]

Code of Ethics

A code of ethics is intended to address how people act within the organization, regardless of whether they are employees, officers, directors, or

7. Nonvoting directors are not considered "directors" for this purpose.

Form 990 Review

The board should ensure there is a policy or defined process for the review of the Form 990. The Form 990 asks if the board has received the Form 990 in advance of its filing. It also asks about the process for reviewing the Form 990, but does not require the full board to review. The board may delegate responsibilities for an in-depth review to a committee; however, it is important that the Form 990 be distributed or made available (such as on a secure board portal) to all board members for review prior to filing with the IRS. In addition, directors should be aware that the Form 990 is not only an important regulatory document, but also important for public relations purposes due to its public availability.

Public Accountability/Disclosure of Documents

A policy on public disclosure should address what documents will be made available to members of the public. Only two documents—the exemption application (Form 1023, 1023 EZ, or 1024) and the informational return (Form 990, 990 EZ, 990 N, or 990 PF)—are required to be made publicly available. That portion of the Form 990 identifying the names and addresses of contributors may be withheld from public inspection (unless the organization is a private foundation).

Copies of the organization's Form 1023 or 1024 and most recent Form 990 are required to be provided to individuals who make a written or in-person request. An in-person request must be honored the same day the request is made. A request made by mail can be responded to within 30 days. The nonprofit may impose a reasonable charge for copies up to the Freedom of Information rate, which currently is 20 cents per page. If the forms are made widely available, such as on the organization's website, the organization is not required to provide copies, but still must make the documents available for inspection.

For nonprofits in existence for a long period of time, it may be difficult to locate the original Form 1023 or 1024. If it cannot be found after reasonable effort, this fact should be explained to any person requesting such forms. Nonprofits that are tax-exempt pursuant to an IRS Group Ruling will not have a Form 1023.

A nonprofit can decide to make other types of information available to the public, such as governing documents and financial information; however, this is not a legal requirement.[10]

Gift Acceptance

This policy has many similarities to the endowment and investment policy because it is intended to address the type of limitations that are acceptable to the organization. There may be situations in which it is not in the best interests of the organization to accept the gift because the limitations are unworkable for the organization. A policy should include a method by which questionable gifts will be presented to the board or a committee thereof for final determination before acceptance.

Contemporaneous Minutes

A policy or guidelines for an organization to follow with regard to minute-taking can be helpful in documenting the organization's legal compliance. Good practices for minutes of boards or board committees include the following:

- include all board resolutions or an accurate summary of each resolution;
- note everyone who attended the meeting, whether in person or by phone, including officers and guests, and note the time of arrival and departure for any directors who are not present for the entire meeting;
- note all persons who abstained or dissented on a vote;
- provide general overview of matters discussed or addressed (it is best not to report verbatim, but instead provide sufficient detail to evidence the board deliberations and discussions on important items);
- major issues, such as approval of major asset purchase or sale, or incurrence of significant debt, should be reflected in a written resolution to avoid later questions about what the board approved;

10. The organization's articles of incorporation is also a public document generally available through the secretary of state's office.

- minutes should be furnished to the board in a timely manner; and
- approval of minutes should occur no later than the next board meeting.

Joint Ventures

This policy may not be necessary or appropriate if the organization does not engage in joint ventures. If a joint venture policy is to be adopted, consideration should be given to the type of joint venture that is expected and the specific issues that might arise for such ventures. If it is determined that such a policy is appropriate, the policy should address safeguards for the organization's tax-exempt status when participating in joint ventures or similar arrangements with nonprofit or for-profit third parties.

ATTORNEY SERVING ON NONPROFIT CLIENT'S BOARD OF DIRECTORS

Attorneys often are requested to serve on nonprofit boards of directors. Given that most nonprofits have limited resources, they may expect an attorney-director to provide some form of legal services on a pro bono basis.

An attorney-director must be mindful of the fiduciary duties imposed on directors of nonprofit organizations, the ethical duties imposed on attorneys, as well as the potential issues that arise as a result of an attorney serving on a nonprofit board. Although there are some risks associated with such service, there are ways that these risks might be managed.

A director has fiduciary duties to the organization. The main duties are the duty of care and the duty of loyalty. In terms of the ethical obligations imposed on attorneys in their representation of clients, Rule 1.7 of the American Bar Association Model Rules of Professional Conduct (Model Rules) provides that an attorney may not represent a client if such representation involves a concurrent conflict of interest. Attorney-directors who provide legal advice to the corporation from time to time should be careful to be clear on when they are acting as an attorney and when they are acting as a board member. An attorney-director may not be covered by the organization's D&O policy for a claim or lawsuit relating to a challenge to a matter on which the director provided legal advice.

Potential Conflicts of Interest for Attorney-Directors

Conflicts can arise for attorneys serving as members of a nonprofit's board of directors because of the duties imposed on nonprofit directors as well as the attorneys' ethical duties to clients as set forth in the Model Rules. As part of the duty of loyalty, a director is required to act in the best interests of the organization, which can include, for example, not using confidential information of the organization to the detriment of the organization. With such a duty to the organization, an attorney's service on the board of directors of a nonprofit might preclude the attorney or the attorney's law firm from being adverse to the organization.

Conflicts also can arise for an attorney-director when the attorney's firm represents a client that is a grant recipient of the nonprofit. To the extent such situations occur infrequently, the organization and attorney-director should be able to handle them by following conflict of interest requirements that are imposed by state statute and the organization's conflict of interest policies.

Other types of conflicts can arise when the attorney-director is serving as the attorney for the nonprofit. ABA Formal Ethics Opinion 98-410 identifies four possible conflict situations, and although the focus of the formal ethics opinion is primarily on for-profit organizations, the rationale can apply to nonprofit organizations as well. The first situation is when the attorney is asked to pursue objectives of the organization that, as a director, the attorney opposed. According to the formal ethics opinion, an attorney must determine whether his or her representation of the organization may be materially limited by the attorney's opposition to the action the organization has decided to undertake such that Model Rule 1.7 precludes the representation. The second situation occurs when an attorney is asked to opine on board actions in which the attorney participated. The third situation described in the formal ethics opinion is when the board is taking action affecting the attorney's law firm, such as when the board is determining whether to retain the law firm. In such a situation, it is important to comply with the applicable conflict of interest procedures and ensure the attorney-director is not part of the decision process. The fourth situation described in the formal ethics opinion occurs when the attorney or attorney's law firm represents the organization in litigation that includes the organization and directors as defendants. Among other things, it notes the need for the organization and directors to have independent representation in any controversy between the organization and its attorneys (including the attorney-director).

Attorney-Client Privilege Waivers

Assuming there is an attorney-client relationship, the attorney-director's dual roles can, in some situations, make it difficult to ensure that the attorney-client privilege protects communications between the attorney and the nonprofit organization. A basic element of the privilege is that the attorney acts as legal counsel rather than as a business advisor to protect communication from disclosure in litigation. In the for-profit context, communications from an attorney-director that involve business issues (as opposed to legal advice) have been held not protected by the attorney-client privilege. The same argument could be made in the nonprofit context.

Although the attorney-director should understand when he or she is acting as legal counsel as opposed to a business advisor, these separate roles may not be clear to nonattorney directors and officers of the organization. The comments to Model Rule 1.7 provide that an attorney must warn a corporate client of the potential loss of the attorney-client privilege when the attorney is also a board member.

Protections for Attorney-Directors

The protections available to directors of nonprofit organizations and attorneys are also available to attorney-directors. In terms of protections for nonprofit directors, the MNCA as well as many states' nonprofit statutes provide a liability shield for directors and officers acting in such capacity. This shield will protect the directors from liability to the organization and its members for money damages unless their conduct is deemed to fall under an exception to the shield.

Directors and officers (D&O) insurance coverage can be helpful in protecting attorneys in their service as directors of a nonprofit organization. In addition, professional liability coverage should provide protection for the attorney-director when acting in the role of the attorney for the organization. Nevertheless, it is important to recognize that professional liability coverage generally does not cover claims arising out of an attorney's service as a director, and D&O policies often limit claims arising solely out of service as a director or officer.

Considerations for Attorneys Serving on Nonprofit Client Boards

Before agreeing to serve as a director or officer of a nonprofit organization, an attorney should review:

- the expectations of the attorney-director regarding legal representation;
- the organization's governance documents and applicable state nonprofit law;
- the organization's D&O liability coverage;
- the attorney's professional liability coverage; and
- the attorney's law firm or employer policies regarding board service.

The attorney also should consider the likelihood the attorney's role as a director will present conflicts in representation of clients that may be adverse to the nonprofit organization.

In accepting a position on the board of directors of a client organization, an attorney-director should provide an explanation of the potential conflicts of interest and how they might preclude the attorney-director from acting as either the director or an attorney on some issues or require safeguards, such as engaging the services of counsel other than the attorney-director or the attorney-director's law firm. It is important to make the other board members aware of the potential conflicts. Moreover, in order to address a potential conflict adequately, an attorney-director should not participate in board or committee deliberations or actions on the relationship of the organization with the attorney.

When an attorney-director speaks to the board as an attorney for the organization, he or she should communicate that fact and remind the board of the methods of preserving the attorney-client privilege.

If the attorney-director agrees to take on a specific, limited representation of the organization, such as preparing restated articles of incorporation or an employment agreement for the executive director, the attorney should make clear—preferably in writing to the organization—the extent of the representation.

An attorney-director should not provide legal representation on a matter outside of the attorney's area of expertise. In that context, the attorney-director should make clear to the board the extent of the attorney's expertise and the fact that any statements made by the attorney with regard to such subject matter are made as a director and not as an attorney to the entity.

KEYS TO EFFECTIVE BOARD SERVICE

Some keys to a well-functioning board include:

- Be clear on board member roles and large board, small board, and fiduciary obligations. (A job description for the board chair, vice chair, and directors in general may be useful.)
- Specify board member qualifications, i.e., minimum standards and specialized areas of expertise.
- Board orientation and education should cover: (1) general information about the organization, including its mission and history; and (2) specific information covering the industry, key areas, legal/industry developments, administrative structure, and identification of key employees.
- Ensure a clear board/management structure through committee charters, corporate organization chart, and powers over or held by affiliates.
- Address board culture emphasizing the need for collegiality, civility, open to questions, respect for group decisions.
- Board focus should be on ensuring major policies applicable to the board, major decisions, and organization compliance with law.

CORPORATE HOUSEKEEPING

There are certain minimum "corporate housekeeping" activities that should take place to maintain effective board functioning and the corporation's status as a distinct entity apart from its board or members.

- **Board Meetings.** There should be regular meetings of the board of directors. A corporation functions through its board of directors, and the board is not effective unless it is meeting. A small board typically can hold meetings under general principles of due process and fair dealing. Procedural rules for deliberative meetings involving large boards, representative bodies, delegate assemblies, and large memberships may benefit from adopting procedural rules in advance.

- **Minutes.** The minutes reflect the activities of the board. If there is ever an issue of what happened at a board meeting, one of the first things that will be reviewed will be the minutes of the meeting. If the minutes do not reflect the deliberations or action of the board, it will be difficult to prove that the board took the action the directors claim were taken.
- **Policies.** It is important for board members to review material policies implemented by the nonprofit corporation and whether they address the significant risks facing the organization.
- **Initial and Continuing Registrations.**
    - **Annual/Biennial Filings (State).** A state typically has an annual or biennial filing that must be made by nonprofit corporations, identifying officers and directors and contact information for the organization. Failure to do so can result in the administrative dissolution of the nonprofit corporation. These forms typically are filed with the appropriate secretary of state's office, but the specific office varies from state to state.
    - **Filings with Attorney General (State).** In some states, additional filings must be made with the state's attorney general for applicable charities.
    - **Tax Filings (Federal and State).** The Form 990 must be filed with the IRS on an annual basis. The Form 990 must be filed as soon as the nonprofit corporation is incorporated (even before the entity obtains its tax-exempt status). The failure to file a Form 990 for three consecutive years can result in a revocation of tax-exempt status. Many states have parallel forms, although some accept copies of the federal forms.

Other Matters Arising in Representation of a Nonprofit

5

SUBSIDIARIES OF NONPROFITS

Some nonprofit corporations will incorporate or otherwise organize subsidiaries for various reasons. From a tax standpoint, a corporate subsidiary (such as a nonprofit corporation) will be subject to federal income tax unless it obtains its own tax-exempt status, whereas the single-member limited liability company generally will be treated as a disregarded entity by the IRS.

Nonprofit Corporation Subsidiaries

A mutual benefit nonprofit corporation might want to establish a nonprofit corporation subsidiary that is a charitable nonprofit corporation with tax-exempt status under section 501(c)(3). This type of entity would have a charitable purpose, such as supporting education related to the trade supported by the mutual benefit corporation. By establishing such a nonprofit subsidiary, it is possible to attract charitable contributions that are deductible as well as obtain grant funding that is restricted to entities with tax-exempt status under section 501(c)(3).

A charitable nonprofit corporation also may establish a nonprofit subsidiary with tax-exempt status under section 501(c)(3) so that it can divide the responsibilities between the two organizations, with one organization being the "operating" entity with a focus on carrying out the mission of the organization, and the other organization being the "fundraising" entity with a focus on generating funds that will support the operating entity. Two organizations might make sense for purposes of separating the assets and liabilities of the two organizations. This may be particularly attractive in the situation in which the fundraising entity has significant assets that otherwise would be at risk of paying liabilities of the operating entity.

Because a nonprofit is not "owned" by anyone, the nonprofit will not own its nonprofit corporation subsidiaries. Instead, the parent nonprofit generally will exert control over the subsidiary nonprofit by either being the sole member of the subsidiary nonprofit with control over such organization, or being able to appoint and remove the board of directors of the subsidiary nonprofit, or both.

For-Profit Corporation Subsidiaries

A nonprofit corporation often will incorporate a for-profit subsidiary for purposes of preventing the activities—that would be part of the for-profit subsidiary—from jeopardizing the tax-exempt status of the nonprofit corporation. For example, the nonprofit may establish a for-profit subsidiary to engage in activities that would result in unrelated business taxable income (UBTI) if engaged in directly by the nonprofit. To the extent there is risk associated with the activities of a for-profit subsidiary, the existence of the for-profit subsidiary can help protect the assets of the nonprofit parent from potential liability. A nonprofit corporation may incorporate a for-profit subsidiary for other purposes, including protecting the parent nonprofit entity from liability for the activities of the subsidiary organization, and providing other avenues of funding through private investment and loans from the U.S Small Business Administration.

In the context of a tax-exempt parent nonprofit corporation and a taxable subsidiary, the IRS will respect the separate status of the subsidiary so long as it engages in an independent, bona fide function and is not a mere instrumentality of the parent. With respect to whether the subsidiary is a mere instrumentality of the tax-exempt parent, the IRS looks to the parent's involvement in, and control of, the day-to-day operations of the subsidiary and the subsidiary's maintenance of corporate formalities, such as regular board meetings. Control through stock ownership or the power to appoint the board of directors will not cause the attribution of the subsidiary's activities to the parent. Furthermore, overlapping directors, officers, or employees of two organizations will not automatically result in attribution of a subsidiary's activities to the parent. Rather, the IRS has stated that, unless the facts provide clear and convincing evidence that the subsidiary is in reality an arm, agent, or integral part of the parent, the activities of the separately incorporated subsidiary cannot ordinarily be attributed to the parent organization.

Limited Liability Company Subsidiaries

The use of a limited liability company as a subsidiary of a nonprofit corporation may be an attractive alternative to the extent the nonprofit is not concerned about the activities of the limited liability company being taxable as UBTI. Under the Internal Revenue Code (IRC), a single-member LLC typically is treated as a "disregarded entity" for purposes of federal income taxes. Instead, the LLC is treated as a division of the parent nonprofit for federal tax purposes. As such, it is not required to file a Form 1023 application for recognition of exemption or a Form 990. An LLC with one or more exempt organization members may elect and establish its own tax-exempt status with the IRS.

The IRS has issued guidance making clear that charitable contributions to a domestic LLC subsidiary of a U.S. tax-exempt (section 501(c)(3)) organization are treated as charitable contributions to the parent tax-exempt organization.[1]

A limited liability company generally can be set up for a profit or nonprofit purpose. There may be situations in which a nonprofit corporation—due to liability concerns—desires to utilize a limited liability company structure.

Other Considerations for Subsidiaries

The mere establishment of a subsidiary organization will not automatically protect the parent organization from the liabilities of the subsidiary.

1. *See* I.R.S. Notice 2012-52.

If there is a failure to follow certain corporate formalities and maintain some separateness of operations, the liabilities of the subsidiary can become the liabilities of the parent organization through such theories as "alter ego" and "veil piercing." The doctrine of piercing the corporate veil can apply to limited liability companies. Nevertheless, whereas in the corporate setting a disregard of corporate formalities can be a key element in a piercing analysis, for limited liability companies such an element can be inapplicable because of the informality of organization and operation is both common and desired.[2]

MERGERS, SALE OF ASSETS, AND SIMILAR TRANSACTIONS

In recent years, there has been an increase in mergers, asset transfers, and affiliations involving nonprofit organizations. These "entity combinations" have been necessary in an environment that has become more challenging for nonprofits to obtain financial support in the form of public and private funding and contributions. The process for pursuing a nonprofit business combination, including use of letters of intent or term sheets, due diligence, and the negotiation and execution of documents to effectuate the combination, is similar to the process used with for-profit entities. Nevertheless, entity combinations involving nonprofits have important differences from their for-profit counterparts because of the unique nature of nonprofits. Below is an overview of common forms of nonprofit corporation entity combinations that highlights some aspects of these transactions that differentiate them from for-profit transactions.

Considerations for Moving Forward with Entity Combinations

An initial step in any entity combination is determining whether such combination makes sense to the nonprofit. The factors that a nonprofit board must take into consideration in such evaluation are similar to those factors a for-profit board considers, including synergies, cost savings, and other efficiencies to be obtained through the combination, workforce issues, and the composition of the surviving entity's board and its officers. Moreover,

2. Revised Uniform Limited Liability Company Act, Comment to § 304.

the fiduciary duties imposed on nonprofit directors in acting on entity combinations are similar to the fiduciary duties imposed on for-profit directors. Still, there are some important differences between for-profit and nonprofit entity combinations. For example, a for-profit board must consider the financial impact an entity combination will have on the entity's owners (such as shareholders in a business corporation). In the context of a charitable nonprofit corporation, the interests of members may be somewhat relevant in a board's consideration of a merger, but such interests are not the overriding concern because members do not have an ownership interest in the nonprofit. The differences between for-profits and nonprofits lead to other unique factors that must be considered by a nonprofit board when evaluating a possible entity combination.

If the proposed combination involves a nonprofit merged out of existence, selling substantially all of its assets, or becoming a "subsidiary" of another entity, a main focus of the nonprofit board likely relates to whether the mission of the entity will continue to be carried on by the surviving entity with adequate resources dedicated to such mission. This may result in a requirement by the nonprofit that the mission of the surviving entity incorporate in some respect the nonprofit's mission. The effect on the beneficiaries, employees, creditors, and other stakeholders (e.g., local community members) of the merging nonprofit should also be evaluated.

Other unique considerations include what will happen to any members of the nonprofit, as well as the proposed use of any institutional funds with donor restrictions (including endowment funds) of the nonprofit.

Similar to the situation involving a for-profit entity combination, as the nonprofit commences discussions with another entity regarding a possible entity combination, a letter of intent or term sheet (typically nonbinding except for limited provisions such as confidentiality) helps structure the proposed transaction and process for the combination. In order to protect the nonprofit, it is important to have a binding confidentiality agreement in place prior to any significant discussions between the parties.

A major difference with entity combinations involving nonprofits is that, unlike a situation where a for-profit entity will seek to make money and ensure the combination results in at least a break-even situation, with the combination of two nonprofits, the survivor may be willing to assume more liabilities than assets to protect the mission, and there may be deferred gifts that will be obtained through a merger that will balance out the debts.

Mergers

The Model Nonprofit Corporation Act, Third Edition (MNCA), and most state nonprofit corporation acts permit a nonprofit corporation to merge with another nonprofit corporation pursuant to a process that is similar to the process required of for-profit entities.[3] A state nonprofit corporation act also may allow a nonprofit to merge with a for-profit entity, such as a for-profit corporation, limited liability company, or limited partnership. In addition, a state nonprofit corporation act may allow a nonprofit to merge with an unincorporated nonprofit association as well as with an entity that is domesticated in another state. Not all state corporation acts permit mergers between such different categories of entities, however. For any merger, it is important to confirm that it is permitted under both the applicable nonprofit corporation statute and the enabling statute for the other entity involved in the merger.

The process for a merger involving a nonprofit corporation is similar to a merger involving a for-profit entity. It typically includes a plan of merger or merger agreement containing the terms of the merger and any appropriate representations and warranties of the merging parties. It also involves the filing of articles or certificate of merger with the appropriate secretary of state office. Regardless of which nonprofit is the surviving entity, it generally is necessary to obtain board of director approval from both nonprofits as well as member approval if the nonprofit has members.

Depending on the type of entity that will be the surviving entity in the merger, there may be unique state law requirements as well as requirements imposed on the nonprofit because of its tax-exempt status. A merger involving a charitable nonprofit is subject to additional requirements if the charitable nonprofit is merged out of existence, and the surviving entity is not a charitable nonprofit. Steps to ensure that the charitable assets or the fair value of such assets of a merged-out entity continue to be used for a charitable purpose. A similar requirement is imposed on entities that have tax-exempt status under section 501(c)(3). Additional requirements under

---

3. Some state nonprofit acts and the MNCA also permit membership exchanges in which a nonprofit corporation, pursuant to a plan of membership exchange, acquires all of the memberships of one or more classes of another nonprofit. *See* MNCA § 11.03.

the Internal Revenue Code are imposed on nonprofits that are private foundations. In addition, some states require a merger be approved by a governmental body, such as the state attorney general or a court. Where there must be action taken to ensure that the fair value of the charitable assets is preserved, a valuation by an independent appraiser is likely necessary.

There are significant benefits with regard to proceeding with a merger as the form of entity combination. Similar to state for-profit entity acts, state nonprofit corporation acts provide that all assets and rights and liabilities of the merged-out (nonsurviving) entity are automatically transferred or assumed by the surviving entity. There also is no need to dissolve the merged-out entity because it no longer exists as a legal entity. In addition, state nonprofit corporation acts often will provide that any bequest, devise, gift, grant, or promise contained in a will or other instrument of donation inures to the surviving entity (assuming that it is also a nonprofit or otherwise qualified to receive such bequests, grants, or other arrangements) unless it is made pursuant to an instrument that specifically provides otherwise.

A main disadvantage to a merger is that the surviving entity inherits all of the liabilities of the merged-out entity, and it is not easily possible to unwind the arrangement if it is later determined that the combination has not resulted in the benefits the parties expected. As a result, it is extremely important as part of the due diligence process to determine what assets and liabilities might be assumed by the surviving entity.

Some state nonprofit corporation acts also permit the consolidation of nonprofits, which is similar to a merger of a nonprofit with another nonprofit. The main distinction between a merger and consolidation is that a consolidation results in both nonprofits effectively merged out of existence with the creation of a new entity. A main disadvantage with proceeding with a consolidation as opposed to a merger is that, in a consolidation, it is necessary to make an application to the IRS if the new entity seeks to have tax-exempt status under section 501(c)(3). Given the similar treatment of mergers and consolidations of nonprofits, more recent state nonprofit corporation acts have dropped the concept of consolidation.

A merger also may result in a surviving organization and a disappearing organization or in the creation of a brand-new organization. The "surviving organization" often undergoes substantial changes, such as change of name and board structure. Nevertheless, it is viewed as the legal continuation of the surviving organization. The surviving and merged organizations must communicate the merger to the IRS in the Form 990 filing. Moreover, if there is to be a new organization created from the merger, it must receive determination from the IRS that it is tax-exempt. If there is any concern about the tax consequences of a proposed merger, consideration should be given to first requesting a private letter ruling from the IRS.[4]

Asset Acquisitions/Sales

Another form of entity combination involves the acquisition or sale of assets of an entity. This might be in the form of a nonprofit acquiring the assets of another nonprofit or a for-profit. Alternatively, the transaction might involve a for-profit acquiring the assets of a nonprofit. The structure of such a transaction is similar to the structure of an acquisition of assets involving for-profit entities. In particular, the selling entity transfers certain identified assets and liabilities to the acquiring entity.

Similar to a merger, the process for the sale of all or substantially all of the assets of a nonprofit is governed by the state nonprofit corporation acts. The MNCA and many nonprofit corporation statutes provide that a sale by a nonprofit of all or substantially all of its assets generally requires approval by the nonprofit corporation's board of directors as well as the members if the nonprofit has members with the authority to vote on such matters.

The form of asset purchase agreement used often is similar to the form used in for-profit transactions and will include a description of the assets transferred, the liabilities assumed, and appropriate representations and warranties regarding such assets and liabilities and the parties. Such agreement likely must also include provisions that are unique to a nonprofit. For instance, in the situation in which a noncharitable entity is acquiring the assets of a charitable entity, the buyer may require that, as a condition of closing, the seller deliver any approvals necessary from state governmental authorities for the sale of the seller's charitable assets.

A significant difference between an acquisition of the assets and liabilities of a nonprofit versus a for-profit can relate to the purchase price. If the acquisition involves two nonprofit entities, it may not be necessary for the

4. *See* I.R.S. Publication 4779, *Facts about Terminating or Merging your Exempt Organization.*

acquiring nonprofit to pay fair market value (or anything) for the assets. Instead, the transaction can be structured as a gift of assets from the selling nonprofit to the acquiring nonprofit. Such gift should be permissible so long as the "selling" nonprofit corporation's creditors are paid in full upon liquidation of the nonprofit. In some cases, the purchasing nonprofit may agree to maintain certain operations of the seller as part of the purchase consideration.

A gift structure is not possible if the nonprofit is acquiring assets from a for-profit entity, or a for-profit entity is acquiring assets from a nonprofit entity. To the extent that a charitable nonprofit is selling its assets to a noncharitable entity, such as a business corporation, similar to the situation in mergers, state nonprofit corporation acts often require that there be fair value paid for the assets. In addition, many states impose requirements that the nonprofit obtain approval from a governmental body (such as the attorney general) or a court in order to proceed with the transaction. In such a situation, it would be important to obtain an independent valuation of the assets as part of the transaction.

A main advantage of an asset transaction is that the acquiring nonprofit is able to be selective in terms of the assets and liabilities it acquires. As a result, it can avoid becoming burdened with the liabilities of the other entity. A main disadvantage is that additional steps might need to be taken in order to complete the transaction. These include obtaining assignments of any relevant revenue-generating agreements, including consents from the other parties to such agreements. In addition, the selling entity remains in existence, and its board must take steps to either wind down its activities and dissolve, or continue its existence. Another disadvantage is that deferred gifts to the selling organization generally are not automatically (by law) transferred to the acquirer.

Parent-Subsidiary Type Arrangements

Nonprofit corporations differ from for-profit entities in that nonprofits have no owners, whereas for-profits have shareholders or other owners. Nonetheless, a parent-subsidiary structure can be structured with nonprofits. The main difference is that the "parent" nonprofit does not own any shares or other interest in the nonprofit. Instead, it is treated as the parent because of the control it has over the other nonprofit. This can be accomplished by the parent nonprofit becoming the sole voting member of the "subsidiary" nonprofit. It also could be accomplished by the parent nonprofit having the right to determine the directors of the subsidiary nonprofit. Another important difference between a nonprofit and for-profit, parent-subsidiary structure is that nonprofit corporations are unable to file consolidated tax returns with the IRS, although it may have consolidated financial statements for auditing purposes. LLCs are consolidated for purposes of the tax return.

The arrangement, which is sometimes referred to as an "affiliation" of nonprofits, can be accomplished by amendments to the articles of incorporation and bylaws of the "subsidiary" nonprofit. These documents would be amended to reflect the "parent" organization either as the sole member (with sole voting rights) of the "subsidiary," or having a right to determine the board of directors of the subsidiary. An amendment to the articles of incorporation or bylaws to create a new parent relationship by the parent corporation becoming the sole member of another nonprofit is also referred to as a "member substitution" transaction.

Because this type of combination or affiliation is similar to a merger or acquisition of assets, parties often enter into some type of affiliation agreement that covers similar topics as those contained in other entity combination agreements. For instance, an affiliation agreement might address any change in activities of the subsidiary nonprofit as well as the composition of the parent's board of directors. Like asset purchase and merger agreements, affiliation agreements also typically include certain representations and warranties about the parties and their operations.

One of the main advantages of a parent-subsidiary type of structure is that the parent does not assume the liabilities of the subsidiary entity. In addition, the affiliation often can be easily accomplished by amending the governance documents of the "subsidiary" entity. This type of structure also is attractive to entities that are not certain about the "permanency" of the arrangement and would like the ability to "unwind" the entity combination if it is subsequently determined that the combination is not working out. The unwinding of the entity combination can be accomplished through amendments to the governing documents to take the parent organization out of the control position of the subsidiary.

A disadvantage to this type of entity combination is that the parties may not achieve the efficiencies that can be obtained through a merger. In particular, there will still be two separate entities that must file their own Form 990s with the IRS. There also will be a need to keep in place two separate boards of directors (although the subsidiary board can be quite small and meet infrequently, assuming that the parent board is addressing issues relevant to the subsidiary). Some organizations that choose to use this type of structure will—through a merger—collapse the subsidiary into the parent at some later point in time when it is determined that the combination should be permanent.

A variation of this structure is the incorporation of a third nonprofit corporation that becomes the sole member (or parent) of the existing nonprofit corporations. This may be attractive to nonprofits that see themselves as "equals" to each other. The advantages to such a structure are similar to the advantages of the parent-subsidiary structure. One disadvantage is that a new nonprofit corporation must be incorporated and likely must obtain tax-exempt status. In addition, the IRS has shown some disfavor to granting tax-exempt status to entities that are merely holding companies with no operations. As a result, it may be necessary to have some activities of the combined nonprofits occurring at the "parent" level. In some cases, the new parent corporation provides administrative services and functions as a supporting organization for tax purposes.

Forms of Less Integrated Affiliations

Although beyond the scope of this book, nonprofits can be involved in other types of arrangements that result in organizations combining their resources to a lesser extent. For instance, two nonprofits may enter into arrangements for joint funding, joint programming, combined services, or other type of joint venture or joint operations. These types of arrangements allow the involved nonprofits to maintain their autonomy while achieving some efficiencies. It is also possible for nonprofits to enter into joint venture arrangements with for-profit entities. Such arrangements raise tax issues that can have an impact on the structure of any joint venture.

Unique Due Diligence Considerations

Similar to entity combinations involving for-profits, due diligence activities are important for entity combinations involving nonprofit corporations. Many of the considerations for a for-profit entity combination are important in due diligence reviews involving a nonprofit entity combination. These include reviewing various information and documents relating to the other entity, including its governance documents (such as articles of incorporation, bylaws, and board policies), financial information (including audited financial statements and any audit reports), contractual arrangements, real and personal property, litigation, regulatory compliance and licensure, insurance coverages, and workforce/employees (and employee benefits).

Still, given the unique nature of nonprofits, there are other factors important to entity combinations involving nonprofits that should be considered as part of the due diligence process. Below is a description of some of these considerations.

- The tax-exempt status of any nonprofit involved in an entity combination is important and should be confirmed through a review of the determination letter issued by the IRS. In addition, there should be a review of recent Form 990 federal tax filings for the nonprofit.
- Many nonprofits are exempt from paying property taxes on their real estate as a result of being a nonprofit. This can mean significant savings to the nonprofit. Because exemption for property tax is not automatically determined on the basis of whether an entity is tax-exempt under the IRC, the parties to an entity combination must consider whether the resulting transaction will jeopardize any existing property tax or other state and local tax exemptions.
- Many nonprofits depend on public and private funding as well as tax-exempt bond financing. The terms of such funding and financings should be reviewed to determine whether the particular form of entity combination will impact the continued existence of such arrangements. For public funding, it generally is necessary to submit a new application for grant funding. In addition, many nonprofits have institutional funds that have restrictions imposed on them by their donors. As noted above, in the context of a merger, any such funds presumptively are transferred to the surviving entity unless there are restrictions that prohibit such transfer. It is important that donor fund restrictions be considered as part of the due diligence process to ensure that a transfer is possible and that the surviving entity is able to honor such restrictions.

- If the entity operates with a license, it likely must obtain a new license from the appropriate licensure authority.
- As described above, an entity combination involving a nonprofit corporation may require approval by the nonprofit's members if it has any. For nonprofits with members, it is important to determine whether such members meet the state nonprofit corporation act's definition of "members." Typically, such definition focuses on individuals or entities that elect part or all of the board of directors. As noted in Chapter 2, a nonprofit may have a group of individuals designated as members who do not have such approval rights. In such circumstances, it may not be necessary to obtain their approval of the merger (or other entity combination) unless the articles or bylaws of the organization mandate such approval.
- Also as described above, if the surviving entity in a combination involving one or more nonprofits results in an entity that is not a charitable nonprofit, it may be necessary to obtain state attorney general or court approval. Such determination should be made as part of the due diligence process.

Summary

A merger, asset transaction, affiliation, or other entity combination involving a nonprofit corporation has many characteristics that are similar to those of an entity combination involving for-profit entities. Nevertheless, an entity combination involving a nonprofit is not a typical M&A transaction and, due to the unique nature of a nonprofit, there are important differences that must be addressed when considering such an entity combination.

DISSOLUTION

Voluntary Dissolution

State nonprofit corporation acts set forth procedures for voluntary and involuntary dissolution of nonprofit corporations that are similar to state for-profit corporation acts. In many states, voluntary dissolution requires the filing of articles of dissolution as well as the development of a plan of dissolution. To accomplish the dissolution, the directors must approve a plan of dissolution indicating to whom the assets owned or held by the corporation will be distributed after all creditors have been paid. At any time after the dissolution is authorized, the nonprofit corporation typically may dissolve by delivering articles of dissolution to the secretary of state.

Voluntary dissolution typically may occur only if approved by the board, the members, if any, and by any person or persons whose approval is required by a provision of the articles for an amendment to the articles or bylaws. State law often will provide that, to the extent a corporation has never elected or appointed directors or members, the incorporator of a corporation is authorized to dissolve a corporation and, to the extent a corporation has directors but no members, the directors are able to voluntarily dissolve the corporation.

Similar to the situation for a for-profit corporation, a dissolved corporation continues its corporate existence, but is not allowed to carry on any activities except those appropriate to wind up and liquidate its affairs, including all of the following: (1) preserving and protecting its assets and minimizing its liabilities; (2) discharging or making provision for discharging its liabilities and obligations; (3) disposing of its properties that will not be distributed in kind; (4) returning, transferring, or conveying assets held by the corporation upon a condition requiring return, transfer, or conveyance, which condition occurs by reason of dissolution in accordance with such condition; (5) transferring, subject to any contractual or legal requirements, its assets as provided in or authorized by its articles of incorporation or bylaws; and (6) doing every other act necessary to wind up and liquidate its assets and affairs.

If the corporation is a public benefit or religious corporation, the distribution of assets may need to occur in a manner in which the charitable purpose of such assets will continue. This typically requires that a corporation distribute assets only to those types of entities described in section 501(c)(3).

In contrast, if the nonprofit corporation is a mutual benefit corporation, and a provision has not been made in its articles or bylaws for the distribution of assets on dissolution, it often is permissible to transfer assets to the nonprofit corporation's members or, if it has no members, those persons to whom the corporation holds itself out as benefitting or serving. This is called a "liquidating distribution" and is not considered a form of private inurement. It may, however, have taxable consequences for the recipient.

Similar to the situation involving a dissolution of a for-profit corporation, dissolution of a nonprofit corporation does not do any of the following: (1) transfer title to the corporation's property; (2) subject its directors or officers to standards of conduct different than those prescribed by the applicable nonprofit act; (3) change quorum or voting requirements for its board or members; (4) change provisions for selection, resignation, or removal of its directors or officers or both; (5) change provisions for amending its bylaws; (6) prevent commencement of a proceeding by or against a corporation in its corporate name; (7) abate or suspend a proceeding pending by or against the corporation on the effective date of the dissolution; or (8) terminate the authority of the registered agent.

In general, state nonprofit corporation acts set forth a process for notifying creditors of both "known claims" and "unknown claims." For known claims against a dissolved corporation, the dissolved corporation generally is required to notify its known claimants in writing of the dissolution at any time after the effective date of the dissolution and provide a specified period (as designated by the state nonprofit corporation act) to provide the detail for all outstanding claims. A claim against the dissolved corporation will be barred if either of the following occurs: (1) a claimant who was given proper written notice does not deliver the claim to the dissolved corporation by the deadline; and (2) a claimant whose claim was rejected by the dissolved corporation does not commence a proceeding to enforce the claim within a certain number of days from the effective date of the rejection notice.

To address unknown claims against a dissolved corporation, the state nonprofit act dissolution provisions may provide for a dissolved corporation to publish notice of its dissolution and request that persons with claims against the corporation present them in accordance with the notice. If the dissolved corporation properly publishes a newspaper notice, the claims generally will be barred if they are not brought within a certain period of time, which generally is longer than the notice period for known claims.

Similar to for-profit corporation statutes, a nonprofit corporation act often will provide that any claim identified prior to the end of the statutory notice period may be enforced to the following extent, as applicable: (1) against the dissolved corporation, to the extent of its undistributed assets; and (2) if the assets have been distributed in liquidation, against any person, other than a creditor of the corporation, to whom the corporation distributed its property to the extent of the distributee's pro rata share of the claim or the corporate assets distributed to such person in liquidation, whichever is less, but the distributee's total liability for all claims shall not exceed the total amount of assets distributed to the distributee.

Administrative Dissolution

State nonprofit corporation acts also provide procedures for administrative dissolution. In general, an administrative dissolution can occur as a result of: (1) a failure of the nonprofit corporation to file its annual or biennial report with the appropriate secretary of state's office; (2) the corporation being without a registered agent or registered office in the state for a certain period of time; (3) the corporation not notifying the secretary of state within a certain period of time that its registered agent or registered office has been changed, that its registered agent has resigned, or that its registered office has been discontinued; and (4) the corporation's period of duration, if any, as provided in its articles of incorporation has expired.

State nonprofit corporation acts typically set forth a process for reinstatement following administrative dissolution. States vary on how long a nonprofit corporation can be administratively dissolved and remain eligible for reinstatement.

Judicial (Involuntary) Dissolution

State nonprofit corporation acts also provide for judicial dissolution. Under section 14.30 of the MNCA, a state court may dissolve a corporation in a proceeding brought by the attorney general if either of the following is established: (1) the corporation obtained its articles of incorporation through fraud; or (2) the corporation has continued to exceed or abuse the authority conferred upon it by law.

Under the MNCA, a state court also may dissolve a corporation in a proceeding brought by certain minimum number of members, or by a director or any person specified in the articles, if any of the following is established: (1) the directors are deadlocked in the management of the corporate affairs, and the members, if any, are unable to break the deadlock; (2) the directors or those in control of the corporation have acted, are acting, or will act in a manner that is illegal, oppressive, or fraudulent; (3) the members are deadlocked in voting power and have failed, for a period that includes at least two, consecutive annual meeting dates, to elect successors to directors whose terms have, or would otherwise have, expired; (4) the corporate assets are being misapplied or wasted; or (5) the corporation has insufficient assets to continue its activities and is no longer able to assemble a quorum of directors or members. (Depending on the nonprofit corporation act, a religious corporation may be able to preclude such an action in its articles or bylaws).

A state court also may dissolve a corporation in a proceeding brought by a creditor, if either of the following is established: (1) the creditor's claim has been reduced to judgment, the execution on the judgment is returned unsatisfied, and the corporation is insolvent; or (2) the corporation has admitted in writing that the creditor's claim is due and owing and the corporation is insolvent.

Finally, a district court may dissolve a corporation in a proceeding brought by the corporation to have its voluntary dissolution continued under court supervision.

Prior to dissolving a corporation, the court is to consider whether: (1) there are reasonable alternatives to dissolution; (2) dissolution is in the public interest if the corporation is a public benefit corporation; or (3) dissolution is the best way of protecting the interests of members if the corporation is a mutual benefit corporation.

A court in a judicial proceeding brought to dissolve a nonprofit corporation may appoint one or more receivers to wind up and liquidate, or one or more custodians to manage, the affairs of the corporation. The court may appoint an individual or a domestic or foreign business or nonprofit corporation authorized to transact business in the state as a receiver or custodian. In appointing a receiver, the court is to describe the powers and duties of the receiver or custodian in its appointing order.

If, after a hearing, the court determines that one or more grounds for judicial dissolution exists, the court typically will enter a decree dissolving the corporation and specify the effective date of the dissolution. After entering the decree of dissolution, the court is to direct the winding up of the corporation's affairs, the liquidation of the corporation, and the notification of its claimants in accordance with the notice provisions for creditors.

Tax Issues Relating to Dissolution

A nonprofit corporation that has tax-exempt status under section 501(c)(3) is required to permanently dedicate its assets for a section 501(c)(3) purpose. This means that, if the organization dissolves, the assets remaining after paying any debts must be distributed for an exempt purpose described in section 501(c)(3), or distributed to the federal government or a state or local government for a public purpose. As a result, if the organizing document provides that the assets would be distributed to members (other than members that are also 501(c)(3) corporations with similar exempt purposes) or private individuals, or for any purpose other than those provided in section 501(c)(3), the organization should amend its organizing document to remove such statements.

Appendix A

Nonprofit Corporation Articles of Incorporation and Bylaws Checklist

ARTICLES OF INCORPORATION

1. For guidance for legal content of Articles of Incorporation, refer to:
   a. Applicable state nonprofit corporation act
   b. Tax exemption requirements
2. Mandatory Provisions
   a. Name of Corporation
      i. Confirm name is available in state of incorporation – check with Secretary of State's office
   b. Purpose of Corporation
      i. To extent nonprofit will seek tax-exempt status, make sure purpose is consistent with tax-exempt status (review IRS requirements)
      ii. Purpose clause should not be treated as "mission statement"
   c. Irrevocable dedication of assets (review IRS requirements)
   d. Name and address of registered agent
   e. Name and address of incorporator
   f. Description of whether nonprofit has "members" (in certain states)

   g. Description of what will happen to assets of nonprofit upon dissolution (in certain states)
   h. Choice of type of nonprofit, i.e., public benefit, mutual benefit, and religious corporations (in certain states)
   i. Designated body with Board powers (in certain states)
3. Permissive Provisions
   a. Names and addresses of initial Board of Directors (required in some states)
   b. Elimination/Limitation of Liability of Directors
      i. In some states, it is necessary to include language in articles of incorporation in order to take advantage of liability shield available to directors and officers
      ii. Provision eliminates or limits the liability of a director to the corporation or its members for money damages
   c. Indemnification
      In some states, it is necessary to include language in articles of incorporation in order to take advantage of broadest indemnification protection available to directors and officers
   d. Provisions relating to managing and regulating the affairs of the Corporation
   e. Defining, limiting, and regulating the powers of the Corporation, the Board of Directors, members, and any class of members
   f. Characteristics, qualifications, rights, limitations and obligations attaching to each or any class of members (often required to be in articles if there will be different membership rights)
   g. Amendments to Articles of Incorporation

BYLAWS

1. For guidance for legal content of Bylaws, look at:
   a. Applicable state's nonprofit corporation act
   b. Charitable solicitation laws
   c. Tax exemption requirements
   d. Sector-specific requirements

2. Subject Areas
   a. If "Members":
      i. Description of qualifications/selection process
      ii. Description of classes of members (if any)
      iii. Dues obligations
      iv. Member representatives
      v. Process for termination/removal of members
      vi. Process for resignation/reinstatement of members
      vii. Ability to transfer membership interests
      viii. Annual/Regular/Special Meetings
         A. Subject matter of annual meeting (such as election of Directors)
         B. Location of meetings
         C. Notice requirements
         D. Process for waiver of notice
         E. Record date
         F. Member list
         G. Conduct of Meetings
      ix. Quorum and voting requirements
      x. Ballot voting
      xi. Written consents
      xii. Electronic notices and voting
      xiii. Proxy voting
      xiv. Voting on mergers, sale of assets, and dissolution
   b. If no "Members"(as defined in the applicable state nonprofit corporation act), will nonprofit still use term "members" to designate donors or other individual entities involved with organization?
      i. If so, include provisions in Bylaws to address any rights of such "members"
   c. Board of Directors
      i. Powers and limitations of Board
      ii. Selection of Board
      iii. Types of Directors, including ex officio Directors (if any)
      iv. Number or range of Directors
      v. Tenure
         A. Staggered terms
         B. Term limits

- vi. Qualifications
- vii. Removal/Resignation/Vacancies
- viii. Regular/Special Meetings
  - A. Location of meetings
  - B. Waiver of Notice
  - C. Director's assent presumed
  - D. Order of business/conduct of meetings
- ix. Quorum/Voting
- x. Meetings by conference telephone
- xi. Unanimous written consent
- xii Electronic communications/actions
- xiii. Compensation (if any)

d. Committees
- i. Board Committees
- ii. Advisory Committees
- iii. Address authority of each Committee

e. Officers
- i. Chair/Vice-Chair
- ii. President/CEO/Senior Executive Officer
- iii. Secretary
- iv. Treasurer
- v. Other officers
- vi. Address authority of each officer
- vii. Removal/Resignation/Vacancies

f. Indemnification
- i. Mandatory
- ii. Permissive
- iii. Advancement of Expenses
- iv. D&O Insurance

g. Miscellaneous Matters
- i. Receipt and disbursement of funds
- ii. Corporate records and reports and inspection rights
- iii. Representation of shares of other corporations

h. Amendments to Bylaws

Appendix B

Tax-Exempt Organization Reference Chart

ORGANIZATION REFERENCE CHART FROM *TAX-EXEMPT STATUS FOR YOUR ORGANIZATION;* INTERNAL REVENUE SERVICE PUBLICATION 557 (REV. JANUARY 2017)

Section of 1986 Code	**Description of Organization**	**General Nature of Activities**
501(c)(1)	Corporations Organized under Act of Congress (Including Federal Credit Unions)	Instrumentalities of the United States
501(c)(2)	Title Holding Corporation for Exempt Corporation	Holding title to property of an exempt organization
501(c)(3)	Religious, Educational, Charitable, Scientific, Literary, Testing for Public Safety, to Foster National or International Amateur Sports Competition, or Prevention of Cruelty to Children or Animals Organizations	Activities of nature implied by description of class of organization

Section of 1986 Code	Description of Organization	General Nature of Activities
501(c)(4)	Civic Leagues, Social Welfare Organizations, and Local Associations of Employees	Promotion of community welfare; charitable, educational, or recreational
501(c)(5)	Labor, Agricultural, and Horticultural Organizations	Educational or instructive, the purpose being to improve conditions of work and to improve products and efficiency
501(c)(6)	Business Leagues, Chambers of Commerce, Real Estate Boards, etc.	Improvement of business conditions of one or more lines of business
501(c)(7)	Social and Recreation Clubs	Pleasure, recreation, social activities
501(c)(8)	Fraternal Beneficiary Societies and Associations	Lodge providing for payment of life, sickness, accident, or other benefits to members
501(c)(9)	Voluntary Employees' Beneficiary Associations	Providing for payment of life, sickness, accident, or other benefits to members
501(c)(10)	Domestic Fraternal Societies and Associations	Lodge devoting its net earnings to charitable, fraternal, and other specified purposes. No life, sickness, or accident benefits to members
501(c)(11)	Teachers' Retirement Fund Associations	Teachers' association for payment of retirement benefits

Section of 1986 Code	Description of Organization	General Nature of Activities
501(c)(12)	Benevolent Life Insurance Associations, Mutual Ditch or Irrigation Companies, Mutual or Cooperative Telephone Companies, etc.	Activities of a mutually beneficial nature similar to those implied by the description of class or organization
501(c)(13)	Cemetery Companies	Burials and incidental activities
501(c)(14)	State Chartered Credit Unions, Mutual Reserve Funds	Loans to members
501(c)(15)	Mutual Insurance Companies or Associations	Provides insurance to members substantially at cost
501(c)(16)	Cooperative Organizations to Finance Crop Operations	Financing crop operations in conjunction with activities of a marketing or purchasing association
501(c)(17)	Supplemental Unemployment Benefit Trusts	Provides for payment of supplemental unemployment compensation benefits
501(c)(18)	Employee-Funded Pension Trust (created before June 25, 1959)	Payment of benefits under a pension plan funded by employees
501(c)(19)	Post or Organization of Past or Present Members of the Armed Forces	Activities implied by nature of organization
501(c)(21)	Black Lung Benefit Trusts	Funded by coal mine operators to satisfy their liability for disability or death due to black lung diseases

Section of 1986 Code	Description of Organization	General Nature of Activities
501(c)(22)	Withdrawal Liability Payment Fund	Provide funds to meet the liability of employers withdrawing from a multiemployer pension fund
501(c)(23)	Veterans Organization (created before 1880)	Provide insurance and other benefits to veterans
501(c)(25)	Title-Holding Corporations or Trusts with Multiple Parents	Holding title and paying over income from property to 35 or fewer parents or beneficiaries
501(c)(26)	State-Sponsored Organization Providing Health Coverage for High-Risk Individuals	Provide health care coverage for high-risk individuals
501(c)(27)	State-Sponsored Workers' Compensation Reinsurance Organization	Reimburse members for losses under workers' compensation acts
501(c)(28)	National Railroad Retirement Investment Trust	Manage and invest railroad retirement assets
501(c)(29)	Consumer Operated and Oriented Plans (CO-OPs)	Consumer-governed, member-run health insurers
501(d)	Religious and Apostolic Associations	Regular business activities. Communal religious community
501(e)	Cooperative Hospital Service Organizations	Perform cooperative services for hospitals
501(f)	Cooperative Service Organizations of Operating Educational Organizations	Perform collective investment services for educational organizations
501(k)	Child Care Organization	Provides care for children
501(n)	Charitable Risk Pools	Pools certain insurance risks of § 501(c)(3) organizations

Section of 1986 Code	Description of Organization	General Nature of Activities
501(q)	Credit Counseling Organization	Credit Counseling Services
521(a)	Farmers' Cooperative Associations	Cooperative marketing and purchasing for agricultural producers
527	Political Organizations	A party, committee, fund, association, etc., that directly or indirectly accepts contributions or makes expenditures for political campaigns

Appendix C

Nonprofit Resources

The general literature on nonprofit boards and corporations is extensive, and this appendix does not purport to cover all titles, particularly in view of the uneven quality of the material currently offered on the market. The following are recommended resources for additional information on issues relating to nonprofit corporations:

Publications

THE MODEL NONPROFIT CORPORATION ACT, THIRD ED. (American Bar Association 2009); William H. Clark, Jr., editor, contains both the Model Act provisions and official commentary.

GUIDEBOOK FOR DIRECTORS OF NONPROFIT CORPORATIONS, THIRD ED. (American Bar Association 2012) provides practical guidance to directors and officers of nonprofit corporations on many topics relating to nonprofit corporations, including fiduciary duties, the use of committees, tax issues, charitable solicitations and fundraising, bankruptcy, and the duties imposed on directors with the investment and use of institutional funds.

NONPROFIT GOVERNANCE AND MANAGEMENT, THIRD ED. (American Bar Association 2011) is a practical guide for executive staff and boards of directors of nonprofit organizations, providing an overview of the basics on nonprofit governance as well as board structure and operations, including 27 samples of important governance forms and guidelines.

Lisa A. Runquist, The ABCs of Nonprofits, 2d Ed. (American Bar Association 2015) provides a basic understanding of nonprofits and the issues facing nonprofits, describes how nonprofit corporations are formed, options for organizational structure, matters relating to the operation of the corporation, and basic tax issues for nonprofits (Spanish-language edition is also available: El ABC de las Organizaciones Sin Fines de Luco).

The Guide to Representing Religious Organizations (American Bar Association 2009) addresses critical issues and risk factors of concern for religious organizations ranging from formation and governance to taxes, fundraising and employment issues, and property rights. It outlines the general requirements of applicable law and highlights areas in which religious organizations receive special consideration under the law.

ABA Coordinating Committee on Nonprofit Governance, The Guide to Nonprofit Corporate Governance in the Wake of Sarbanes-Oxley (American Bar Association 2005) provides a basic overview of the provisions of the leading Sarbanes-Oxley reforms and discusses their relevance to nonprofit organizations, as well as describes related governance structures, processes, and procedures that have been recognized as "good governance practices."

Bruce R. Hopkins has written several excellent treatises on tax-exempt organizations, including The Law of Tax-Exempt Organizations (John Wiley & Sons, Inc. 11th ed 2015) (with annual updates).

Michael I. Sanders, Joint Ventures Involving Tax-Exempt Organizations (John Wiley & Sons, Inc. 4th ed 2013) (with annual updates), is an excellent treatise on legal issues on joint ventures involving nonprofits.

Jack B. Siegel, A Desktop Guide for Nonprofit Directors, Officers, and Advisors: Avoiding Trouble While Doing Good (John Wiley & Sons, Inc. 2006), provides a detailed analysis of legal issues relevant to board members.

The American Law Institute is working on a project, Restatement of Law - Charitable Nonprofit Organizations, to draft legal principles for the nonprofit sector, including principles relating to governance and the duties of governing boards and individual fiduciaries. Drafts of *the Restatement* are available from ALI <www.ali.org>.

Periodicals

Periodicals focusing on the nonprofit sector include the following:

The Chronicle of Philanthropy, a newspaper focusing on the nonprofit world (*see* website at <www.philanthropy.com>). The *Chronicle* publishes annually their *Non-Profit Handbook*, with lists of books, periodicals, software, Internet sites, and other resources, organized by subject matter (such as "Advocacy," "Boards," and "Fund-Raising").

Don Kramer's Nonprofit Issues, a national newsletter reporting on tax and other legal developments affecting nonprofit organizations.

Bruce Hopkins' The NonProfit Counsel, published by John Wiley & Sons, a monthly newsletter that provides analysis of current developments in tax and related law for nonprofit organizations and their professional advisors.

The Nonprofit Times, a business publication directed to nonprofit management, with 12 monthly editions plus bi-monthly special editions on direct marketing and financial management, and an annual nonprofit salary survey (for information and selected articles, *see* <www.nptimes.com>).

Useful websites and organizations

A reader interested in pursuing further material in this area may consult the following organizations and their websites:

The IRS website <www.irs.gov> has a section focused on charities and nonprofits that contains extensive information on compliance with tax-exempt requirements.

The GuideStar website <www.guidestar.org> is produced by Philanthropic Research, Inc., and contains a database of information from the Form 990s of over 700,000 U.S. nonprofit organizations.

Many states' secretary of state websites and attorney general websites contain useful information for nonprofit organizations. Examples include the California Attorney General Charity Portal <http://caag.state.ca.us/charities>, the Illinois Attorney General Charity Portal <www.ag.state.il.us/charities/reg_reports.html>, and Iowa Secretary of State website <www.sos.state.ia.us/business/nonprofits/index.html>.

BoardSource, <www.boardsource.org>, which has an extended bibliography on topics relevant to nonprofit boards.

Charity Navigator <www.charitynavigator.org/> provides comparison information on thousands of charitable organizations and other information, including executive compensation studies.

The Uniform Law Commission maintains a website of uniform laws relating to nonprofits, which includes the Uniform Prudent Management of Institutional Funds Act, the Uniform Unincorporated Nonprofit Association Act, the Revised Uniform Unincorporated Nonprofit Association Act, and the Model Protection of Charitable Assets Act, at <www.uniformlaws.org>.

The National Council of Nonprofit Associations <www.councilofnonprofits.org> is a network of state and regional associations of nonprofit organizations, developed to provide nonprofits with services, peer support, and a mechanism for collective advocacy.

Various states have nonprofit associations and resource organizations that maintain websites with resource information specific to the state. Examples include the Minnesota Nonprofit Council <www.minnesotanonprofits.org>, the Larned A. Waterman Iowa Nonprofit Resource Center <https://inrc.law.uiowa.edu, inrc.continuetolearn.uiowa.edu>, and the New York Council on Nonprofits <http://www.nycon.org>. The National Council on Nonprofits maintains a directory of state nonprofit associations.

The Nonprofit Organizations Committee of the Business Law Section of the American Bar Association maintains a website <http://apps.americanbar.org/dch/committee.cfm?com=CL580000> that contains various materials, including the text of the Model Nonprofit Corporation Act, Third Edition, and links to nonprofit articles.

The Public Counsel Law Center includes sample Form 990 policies and analysis at <www.publiccounsel.org/useful_materials?id=0025>

The Charity Channel website, <www.charitychannel.com>, provides a wide range of discussion forums on nonprofit topics.

The Independent Sector provides information on and promotes the range of nonprofit organizations that comprise America's independent sector.

See <www.independentsector.org>. In 2004, the Independent Sector convened the Panel on the Nonprofit Sector. This resulted in several publications, including the *Principles for Good Governance and Ethical Practice: A Guide for Charities and Foundations* (2007), which contains 33 practices designed to support board members and staff leaders of every charitable organization as they work to improve their own operations. This publication, as well as other related publications of the Panel on the Nonprofit Sector, is available on the Independent Sector website.

Index

A

B

G

I

O

V

W